T0063639

The Deacon Ministry Handbook

Paul R. Badgett • Alan Dodson • Todd Gray
Rick Howerton • Andy McDonald • Larry J. Purcell
Stephen C. Rice • Alan Witham

The Deacon Ministry Handbook

A PRACTICAL GUIDE
FOR SERVANT LEADERSHIP

B&H
PUBLISHING
BRENTWOOD, TENNESSEE

978-1-0877-6688-1

Published by B&H Publishing Group
Brentwood, Tennessee

Dewey Decimal Classification: 262.1
Subject Heading: DEACONS / LAITY / SERVANTHOOD, CHRISTIAN

Cover design and illustration by Brian Bobel.

3 4 5 6 7 8 9 10 • 27 26 25 24 23

About the Authors

Dr. Paul R. Badgett

Dr. Paul R. Badgett has been the East Regional consultant for the Kentucky Baptist Convention since 2014. Prior to serving at the Kentucky Baptist Convention, Paul was pastor of three Kentucky Baptist churches over a period of twenty-four years. Paul is a strong advocate of mission support through the Cooperative Program of the Kentucky Baptist Convention and has a desire to lead churches to better church health within the East Region of his state. He has received degrees from Eastern Kentucky University (BS), Luther Rice Seminary (MDiv), and Liberty Baptist Theological Seminary (DMin). Paul has one adult daughter, and he and his wife Regina currently reside in Flatwoods, Kentucky.

Dr. Alan Dodson

Dr. Alan Dodson is husband to Amy, father to Allistair and Andrew, trained at The Southern Baptist Theological Seminary (from which he received the Francisco Preaching Award) and New Orleans Baptist Theological Seminary. He currently serves as regional consultant for the South Region of the Kentucky Baptist Convention.

Dr. Todd Gray

Dr. Todd Gray is the executive director-treasurer of the Kentucky Baptist Convention. He has served with the Kentucky Baptist Convention for ten years, three of which in his current role. Before joining the KBC staff, he served as senior pastor of three churches over a period of twenty years in Kentucky and Indiana. He completed both a masters of divinity and a doctor of ministry degree at The Southern Baptist Theological Seminary in Louisville.

Rick Howerton

Rick spent thirteen years as the small group/discipleship specialist at Lifeway Church Resources, three years with NavPress as their small group specialist, five years as the Kentucky Baptist Convention, church consultant for the South Central Region of Kentucky. Rick presently serves as the central groups pastor for Lakepointe Church in Rockwall, Texas. He has been a church planter, pastor, groups pastor, campus minister, teaching pastor, and church consultant. He is a highly sought after trainer and speaker, and is the author of multiple books and Bible studies.

Andy McDonald

Andy McDonald previously served in four churches over a span of twenty-six years, primarily as student minister or a combination role of student and discipleship. He has served eight years with the Kentucky Baptist Convention, six as an evangelism strategist and now as a regional consultant for the North Central Region.

Andy is a graduate of William Tyndale Bible College (BA) and The Southern Baptist Theological Seminary (MA).

Dr. Larry J. Purcell

Larry J. Purcell earned a PhD in leadership, served as a professor at both The Southern Baptist Theological Seminary and Southeastern Baptist Theological Seminary and as a church pastor for more than twenty years before coming to the Kentucky Baptist Convention as a church consultant.

Dr. Stephen C. Rice

Dr. Stephen C. Rice is the team leader of the Church Consulting & Revitalization Team at the Kentucky Baptist Convention. Before coming to the Kentucky Baptist Convention, he served as senior pastor of four Kentucky Baptist churches. Steve is a graduate of Morehead State University (BA), Luther Rice Seminary (MDiv), and Mid-America Baptist Theological Seminary (DMin).

Alan Witham

Alan Witham served as a senior pastor for nineteen years leading three churches in revitalization. He has served for twenty-two years as a consultant helping churches take steps that lead to greater health and revitalization. Alan Witham is a graduate of Campbellsville University (BA) and The Southern Baptist Theological Seminary (MDiv).

Contents

Foreword

Dr. Todd Gray

Some of the most godly and faithful followers of Jesus I know are deacons. In my nearly thirty years of Christian ministry leadership, deacons have often encouraged me when I was down, corrected me when I was wrong, or challenged me when I was not seeing the whole picture. I recall deacons who were soul winners, prayer warriors, faithful servants, and many who provided kind and consistently wise counsel. Those deacons lived out much of the content of *The Deacon Ministry Handbook*.

This book is written by ministry practitioners who know and love the local church and who also respect and value the office of deacon. *The Deacon Ministry Handbook* is a handbook, a heart book, and a health book. It is a handbook in that so many of the situations that will be encountered by a local church deacon are described and addressed in this work. It is a heart book in that it will show deacons how to minister in a way that honors their pastor and their local church while all the time demonstrating love to Christ. It is a health book in that if its counsel is followed, the pastor, church, and deacons can enjoy great ministry health.

Readers of *The Deacon Ministry Handbook* will receive instruction ranging from the selection of deacons from among the congregation, to the ordination of deacons to highlight the value of their role, to the organization of deacons for effective ministry. I pray that this book will be of great value not only to local church deacons but also to the churches and pastors they serve.

Preface

Dr. Stephen C. Rice

The office of deacon is still relevant and biblical in the twenty-first century. Although the emphasis on the office of elder has increased in Baptist congregations, most Baptist churches still need and honor the office of deacon.

When I consider my years in the pastorate, I think of the men with whom the Lord surrounded me. God placed men in the office of deacon who encouraged me, challenged me, advised me, and prayed for me. These men were partners in the ministry of the gospel, they were brothers in Christ, and they were friends when I needed them most. I cherish them and count it a special privilege to have served with them and to have personally served as a deacon early in life.

Many good deacon resources exist, but few are recent and updated. The authors of this resource work regularly with deacons, and they believe deacons play a crucial role in the success of the local pastor and church. We wrote *The Deacon Ministry Handbook* to provide concise, practical guidance to pastors and deacons. Our combined ministry knowledge has produced a tool that can benefit every pastor and deacon in Kentucky and across the Southern Baptist Convention.

How to Use This Resource

The purpose of *The Deacon Ministry Handbook* is to give concise guidance to pastors and deacons. This book serves as a reference guide as well as a training manual. When a question arises, check the contents page to locate the answer to your question. There you will find practical guidance related to your question.

Another way to use the book is as a training manual for new or seasoned deacons. Reading one chapter prior to each meeting, then discussing the content is an effective way to equip seasoned, new, and future deacons.

CHAPTER 1

Deacon Qualifications

Dr. Alan Dodson

New Testament Qualifications for Deacons

For servants in His church, God is concerned not merely with *what* they do but also with *who* they are. In other words, character counts and morality matters. When the need for congregational servants arose in Acts 6, the first instructions about choosing them contained qualifications. Further, when the apostle Paul instructed his protégé Timothy about church management, inspired by the Holy Spirit, he articulated nine qualifications for those who serve in a church's diaconate. From the outset of this resource, let's observe each of the qualifications from Acts 6 and 1 Timothy 3. Remember, the one who allows the Holy Spirit to develop these characteristics within him will find it much easier to serve. The *who* comes before the *what*.

Take a moment to read carefully the two important passages where the deacon's qualifications are clearly denoted.

> Brothers and sisters, select from among you seven men of good reputation, full of the Spirit and wisdom, whom we can appoint to this duty. (Acts 6:3 CSB)

> Deacons, likewise, should be worthy of respect, not hypocritical, not drinking a lot of wine, not greedy for money, holding the mystery of the faith with a clear conscience. They must also be tested first; if they prove blameless, then they can serve as deacons. Wives, likewise, should be worthy of respect, not slanderers, self-controlled, faithful in everything. Deacons are to be husbands of one wife, managing their children and their own households competently. (1 Tim. 3:8–12 CSB)

"Good Reputation"

The first lay servants of the New Testament had to have a good reputation. As you will read later, these men were called out to help the church navigate through a serious fellowship problem. If they did not have a trustworthy reputation, they would have only exacerbated the issue. Likewise, deacons today should be men of good reputation both in and out of the church. Church members should have no doubts that the men who serve them are worthy of their respect.

"Full of the Spirit and Wisdom"

Being "full of the Spirit" may be the most important qualification of a deacon. If one is full of the Holy Spirit, he will have a *good reputation*, spiritual *wisdom*, and be able to fulfill each of the moral qualifications set forth in 1 Timothy 3:8–12. Because of the critical nature of this qualification, let's be sure to understand what it means.

As a believer, at the moment of his new birth, the deacon received a wonderful birth gift in the indwelling of the Holy Spirit. Romans 8:9 says, "You, however, are not in the flesh, but in the Spirit, if indeed the Spirit of God lives in you. If anyone does not have the Spirit of Christ, he does not belong to him" (CSB). Could it be any clearer? The Holy Spirit comes to live within each Christian. Paul stresses that if one does not have the Spirit, he does not belong to Jesus. So the Christian never has to ask, "Do I have the Spirit?" The appropriate question is, "Am I filled with the Spirit who lives within me?"

Notice the final phrase of Ephesians 5:18: "Be filled by the Spirit." The verb "be filled" is interesting. It means for an object to be so completely filled that no room is left empty. Imagine holding in one hand an empty glass and in the other a pitcher of water. As you begin to fill the glass with the water, you watch the level rise. At one point the glass is one-third full, then two-thirds. As you continue to pour the water to the point that the glass is so full another drop would make the water begin to spill over the rim, at that moment the glass would be so full that no space in it would remain empty. A. B. Simpson said this filling "does not mean to have a measure of the Holy Spirit, and to know a good deal of Christ, but to be wholly filled with, and possessed by, the Holy (Spirit), and utterly lost in the life and fullness of Jesus."[1]

The verb "be filled" is written in the present tense. That feature indicates continued action. In other words, while the Spirit indwells the believer at the moment of redemption, the filling of the Spirit must be repeated. When one is full of the Spirit, he is not full of himself. Deacon, are you serving as one full of the Spirit, or are you serving in the flesh? Perhaps you should take a moment now, confess to the Lord your sins, and ask for a fresh filling of the Holy Spirit. When you are filled, you will have no problem serving your church and meeting all other personal requirements.

"Worthy of Respect"

Shifting out attention from Acts 6 to 1 Timothy 3, we see the remaining New Testament qualifications for deacons. This list of nine requirements speaks to the moral character of deacons. First, a deacon is to be a man "worthy of respect." His actions and reactions command the respect of those he serves.

"Not Hypocritical"

The Greek word translated as *hypocritical* literally means "double tongued." A man given to hypocrisy is prone to say one thing to one person and something else to another. A deacon must give a singular report to all the people he serves. Double-talk will render him disrespected.

"Not Drinking a Lot of Wine"

This is a prohibition of drunkenness. With the proclivity toward all types of addictions in today's culture, the church must encourage sober living and help those in the clutches of insobriety. Scripture is replete with cautions toward strong drink and drunkenness. Servant leaders must set the example in this area. Further, how can a man serve the body of Christ when his thinking is clouded by substance abuse?

"Not Greedy for Money"

Deacons are not to use their positions as a means of material gain. The only motive a man should have to serve as a deacon is God's calling him to do so through his church. Deacon service should never be seen as a way to improve one's status in the community. Many outside the church are skeptical of the church's handling of finances. If those people ever become suspicious of church leaders' motives, it could severely damage the church's witness.

"Holding the Mystery of the Faith with a Clear Conscience"

Doctrine matters! Servant leaders in the church should consider "the faith that was delivered to the saints once for all" (Jude 3 CSB) as fundamental, not incidental. This characteristic describes a man who wholeheartedly believes proper biblical teachings. The deacon should not only possess biblical convictions; he must live them. In addition to being a student of the Scriptures with hearty Bible intake, studying doctrinal statements such as *The Baptist Faith and Message* will aid the deacon in "holding the mystery of the faith." As he holds clear biblical doctrine, he must be careful to live it out. People see a deacon's behavior, not his perceptions.

"Tested" and "Blameless"

Regarding these components of a man's morality, the deacon must be tested and blameless. The idea of being tested means that over a period of time, as a man has walked through various circumstances and trials, his character has been proven. Observers should find a deacon's life journey to be blameless. The Greek word translated as *blameless* literally means "unaccused." It means that when the church calls a man to serve as a deacon, his conduct does not fall under accusation in regard to these qualifications. As David Guzik says, "A man demonstrates his fitness for office in the church by his conduct. Deacons are more recognized than appointed."[2]

Godly Wife

Although the Greek word translated at "wives" in 1 Timothy 3:11 can also be translated as *women*, it seems to fit the context and flow of the writing to translate it as *wives*. Notice that immediately following verse 11, Paul continues to discuss the deacon's home life in verse 12. In keeping with this translation, Paul gives expectations of married deacons' wives. They are to "be worthy of respect, not slanderers, self-controlled, [and] faithful in everything." The phrase "worthy of respect" means the same thing as in verse 8. Just as the deacon's life commands the respect of others, if he is married, so should his wife's.

The word translated as *slanderers* literally means "diabolic." It is based on the same word often used to describe Satan. It means that the deacon's wife cannot be known for backbiting, discrediting, or gossiping about others. "Self-controlled" means the deacon's wife is in control of her thoughts, words, and deeds. Finally, "faithful in everything" means that her life demonstrates ongoing commitment to the Lord.

"Husband of One Wife"

Among the qualifications, this one is the most discussed and, frankly, the most debated. What does it mean that *deacons are to be husbands of one wife*? To begin our discussion, let's try to understand the phrase Paul uses. The literal translation of the text is that deacons are to be one-woman men. In other words, each married deacon is required to be singularly devoted to one wife.

When trying to understand Scripture, it important to understand not only the words and phrases used in the text but also the context in which the original recipient ministered. Remember, Paul first sent this letter to Timothy, who was pastoring in Ephesus. A primary rule of interpretation is that the biblical text cannot say now what it did not say then. So let's keep in mind the words and their context as we explore what they meant then and mean today.

A HUSBAND

Some Bible interpreters have approached this text so wood-enly literal that they think a man is not qualified to serve as a deacon unless he is currently married. Therefore, they would argue that no single man—whether a bachelor, divorcee, or widower—is qualified to serve as a deacon. This is not likely what Paul had in mind. Again, this is a list of the attributes of a man of a high moral caliber. A man's current marital status is hardly indicative of his morality. Further, with this understanding, both Paul and Jesus could not have served as deacons.

Not a Polygamist

Other Bible interpreters have thought this phrase prohibits a polygamist from serving as a deacon. Context helps us understand that such an interpretation is not accurate. While polygamy is seen in the Old Testament, it was not a feature of the Roman culture that dominated the first century. Besides, a man living with a harem would not have been accepted into the church.

One Wife for Life

The one-wife-for-life view prohibits men from serving as deacons if they are remarried widowers or divorcees. Regarding the remarried widower, nothing about this phrase would prohibit him from serving as a deacon. As far as divorce, Paul was familiar with the Greek term for it. In fact, he used it repeatedly when he discussed the principles for marriage in 1 Corinthians 7. Had the Holy Spirit inspired him to discuss divorce in the context of 1 Timothy 3, he would have certainly used the term.

A One-Woman Man

Now we circle back to the literal translation of the phrase. What does it mean to be *a one-woman man*? Simply put, the married deacon is to possess a demonstrated devotion to his wife. A womanizer is not qualified to serve as a deacon. A man whose life demonstrates a flippant view of matrimony—manifested in a series of unbiblical divorces and remarriages—is not qualified to serve as a deacon. A *one-woman man* who has been tested has proven that he takes his marriage seriously.

Good Managers of Children and Household

"Managing their children and their own households competently" means that the married deacon with children is a capable godly leader of his family. He is being asked to serve the household of God. If his personal household is out of order, he will not be able to serve the church as he should.

CHAPTER 2

The Deacon's Role

Alan Witham

Where does one go to get a true picture of the role of a deacon? The Bible is our sole source of authority when it comes to defining and understanding the role of deacon. While most would agree with the previous statement, other sources of authority tend to shape the definition and role of deacon in some churches.

For some, the traditions and practices of the past, based not on Scripture but on a false concept of the role of deacon, have shaped the current understanding of their role. An example of this is when we hear, "This is the way deacons have functioned in our church for years." This "way" often looks more like administrators or overseers than servants and ministers.

For some, the experiences of their past have shaped the role of deacon. An example is a church that has had a history of pastoral turnover every few years, and between pastorates the primary leadership mantle fell to deacons to fill the gap. When those primary leadership roles were not viewed as interim, they were carried over even when the next pastor arrived.

What does the Bible say about the role of deacon?

The previous chapter touched on the definition of *deacon* as seen in Scripture. It referred to the fact that the Greek term for "deacon" is *diakonos* which means "servant."

If deacons are by definition servants, their role flows out of that definition. A deacon's role is one of serving. Servants are chosen by God and His church to serve. Servants who do not serve are nothing more than a contradiction.

How then are they to serve? Since the Bible is our sole source of authority for deacon ministry, let's look at Acts 6 to see how deacons served in the New Testament.

How Deacon's Serve

Deacons serve by helping the church navigate conflict in healthy ways.

> And in those days, when the number of the disciples was multiplied, there arose a murmuring of the Grecians against the Hebrews, because their widows were neglected in the daily ministration. (Acts 6:1 KJV)

Healthy churches experience conflict, navigate it in healthy, biblical ways, and become stronger on the other side of it. The early church described in Acts 6 is a case in point. The church was healthy and growing. It experienced conflict. However, the apostles along with the deacons worked through it, and afterward the church grew even more (Acts 6:7). What had the potential for church division resulted in church multiplication. Every new conflict in your church has the potential for either of these two. The determining factor is how the people of the church and, in particular, church leaders choose to address it.

The conflict that arose stemmed from some widows who were being neglected in the daily distribution of food. Their needs were not being met. They were both hungry and angry. In response to these complaints and this conflict, deacons were selected. Their godly wisdom along with their servant mindset led to addressing this conflict well.

One of the greatest differences between healthy churches and unhealthy churches is that unhealthy churches navigate conflict in nonbiblical ways. The result is often division rather than reconciliation and growing levels of health.

As a deacon, you play a vital role in either contributing to the ongoing health or lack thereof in your church when it comes to addressing conflict. People in the church often approach deacons describing a conflict they have with another member in the church. Sometimes the unspoken expectation is for you to shoulder the responsibility of solving their conflict for them. You will be tempted to take on that responsibility for them. Your greatest need on the other hand is to encourage them to talk to the person they have conflict with. Much of the conflict that escalates in church is because people talk *about* each other instead of talking *to* each other. When people approach you as a deacon, encourage them to talk to the person with whom they have an issue. This practice is applying the wisdom of Matthew 18 to their situation. Good questions to ask people in this setting include: "Have you talked to them about this? Would you be willing to talk to them about this?" If the answer is no to either or both of those questions, help them see that until they talk to the person with whom they have issues, they will never resolve the conflict. Deacons can contribute to the health of their congregation by discipling people to discuss things with one another.

Reflect on the Following Questions

In what ways am I helping my church address and work through conflict in biblical, healthy ways?

Do I model the practice of Matthew 18 and talk with the people I have conflict with?

Do I encourage people who approach me to talk with the people they have conflict with?

Do I tend to avoid conflict?

In what ways do I need to grow in this role responsibility as a deacon?

Deacons serve by engaging in shared ministry with the pastor.

Deacons shared ministry included ministry to widows, thus ensuring that all were fed and ministered to. This freed up the apostles to serve in ways that expressed their calling and major area of responsibility.

Then the twelve summoned the multitude of the disciples and said, "It is not desirable that we should leave the word of God and serve tables. . . . But we will give ourselves continually to prayer and to the ministry of the word." (Acts 6:2, 4 NKJV)

Rather than expecting the apostles to carry out the ministry to widows, the deacons were selected to be responsible for this while the apostles gave their attention to prayer and preaching the Word.

When ministry is shared by pastor and deacons, the church functions at its greatest potential. When the pastor is expected to be the doer of all ministry and others watch, the church suffers and functions at less than its full capacity.

One way to engage in shared ministry is to ask your pastor regularly, "What can I assist you with this week?" or "How can I help you?" You can engage in pastoral care to families or serve on a ministry team that provides the help that complements the ministry of the church and pastor.

Reflect on the Following Questions

What am I doing to assist my pastor in freeing him to devote more time to prayer, preaching, and equipping people for ministry?

What did I do last month to help my pastor?

What ministry am I involved in or leading in the life of the church?

In what ways am I a partner in ministry with my pastor?

Am I a cheerleader who cheers my pastor on from the sidelines as I watch him do ministry? Or am I a team player who serves alongside him engaging in ministry with him?

Deacons serve by meeting needs within the church and community.

The need the first deacons met in Acts 6 was feeding and taking care of widows. "Therefore, brethren, seek out from among you seven men of *good* reputation, full of the Holy Spirit and wisdom, whom we may appoint over this business" (Acts 6:3 NKJV). As deacons serve, they do so for a purpose: to meet the needs of people in the church and in the community.

A healthy exercise is to brainstorm and discuss the following two questions:

What needs do we see in our church that are not being met by any other ministry in the church?

What needs do we see in our community that are not being met by any other church or gospel-centered ministry?

Once prayerful consideration has been given to these questions, deacons should prayerfully consider this question: What need or needs is God calling us to meet in our church and/or community?

Deacons cannot meet all the needs that exist in the church and community, but they should meet those that are of utmost importance and the ones God is leading them to address.

Reflect on the Following Questions

What needs do our deacons meet currently?

If our deacons were no longer deacons, would anyone notice? What needs would go unmet?

If someone asked you, "What does a deacon do?," what would be your response?

Deacons serve by helping the church maintain a healthy balance between in-reach and outreach.

Then the word of God spread, and the number of the disciples multiplied greatly in Jerusalem, and a great many of the priests were obedient to the faith. (Acts 6:7 NKJV)

The word *then* is important in verse 7. It implies that once deacons were selected and began sharing ministry with the apostles and meeting real needs, then the church grew even more. The church grew in part due to a shared ministry approach. The church functioned at an even greater capacity than before.

The church also grew in large part due to the evangelistic zeal and lifestyle of the deacons and apostles. In Acts 8:26 and following, one of these faithful deacons is highlighted witnessing to an Ethiopian eunuch. It says of Philip in verse 35, "Then

Philip opened his mouth, and beginning at this Scripture, preached Jesus to him" (NKJV).

The deacons of Acts 6 ministered to needs within the church. This is called in-reach. They also shared the gospel regularly with people in the community. This is called outreach or evangelism. The deacons along with the apostles continued to hold high the name of Jesus, and they championed the practice of sharing the good news of Jesus with others.

Reflect on the Following Questions

In what ways do I practice evangelism in my daily life?

When was the last time I had a gospel conversation with a lost person?

How often do I invite people who are unsaved and unchurched to attend our church?

Do our deacons continue to hold high the value and practice of evangelism?

Deacons serve by organizing for effective ministry.

Organization is a lot like your digestive system. When it works, you hardly notice it. When it doesn't work, it is all you notice. Some deacon bodies are not effective. They lack purpose and organization. They are deacons in name only. Others are effective, intentional, and organized.

Here are some ways deacons can organize and thus have an intentional plan for effective ministry.

Deacon Family Ministry

The Deacon Family Ministry Plan is a plan through which the deacons can join the pastor and church staff in ministering to the physical, spiritual, and emotional needs of each church member and family. Church families are divided into groups of ten or more. Each group of families is then assigned to a deacon who will minister to them over a period of time.

A part of each deacons meeting is spent praying about specific needs of families and in rejoicing over needs met and victories won. Another part of the meeting may be used in developing a deacon's skills in ministering to family needs.

A deacon serves families through this plan in the following ways:

- *Visiting with assigned families.*
- *Witnessing to unsaved family members.* One of the deacon's chief concerns is that every member of his assigned families knows Christ as Savior.
- *Rejoicing with families.* Deacons will share in the joy of persons they serve when they celebrate important events or accomplishments in their lives (birthdays, anniversaries, etc.).
- *Being a friend.* As a deacon listens to troubles and concerns, people will know someone cares.
- *Giving support in times of crisis.* Sometimes a deacon can help persons weather a crisis by listening and giving support. Other times a deacon will know someone else or a community agency that can help.

- *Answering questions about faith or about the church or denomination.*
- *Helping people know and have fellowship with other members and families in the church.*
- *Helping people find ways to serve in and through the church.* Deacons can watch for opportunities for members of their group to use the talents, skills, and abilities God has given them.
- *Praying for and praying with families.*

In the Deacon Family Ministry Plan, every member and every family have a deacon. The more effectively the plan works in the church, the closer the church will come to being a real family in Christ. Congregational cooperation will help make the plan work.

Deacons Ministering through Sunday School Classes

This organizational plan helps deacons partner with staff to help shepherd manageable groups of people. As a church reaches 150 to 200, it becomes increasingly difficult for one pastor or the staff to be the primary pastoral caregivers. Thus there is a need for deacon ministry through the Sunday school to help the staff shepherd the entire congregation.

Deacons are assigned to a particular Sunday school class as their primary ministry role. They work in partnership with the Sunday school teacher to select class care group leaders (one for every six people enrolled) and an outreach leader, thus organizing the class for maximum effectiveness in pastoral care and outreach through the Sunday school. The deacon's primary pastoral care assignment is caring for the Sunday school teacher, assistant teacher, care group leaders, and outreach leaders.

Deacon-Led Ministry Teams

This organizational model selects deacons with leadership and organizational skills to lead a ministry team. They would lead a team that fits their giftedness and passion. Other deacons who might not feel qualified to lead a ministry team could assist and serve on a team. This model invites other laypersons to join deacons in serving in a particular ministry. A church might have a hospital visitation team led by a deacon with three to ten other laypersons serving on the same team. Teams would be started and put in place after prayerfully addressing the question: What need is God calling us as deacons to lead out in meeting?

Gift-Based Deacon Teams

This organizational model puts in place ministry teams that are expressions of the giftedness and passion of the deacons and meet real and currently unmet needs in the church or community. Deacons serve on a ministry team in an area where they feel gifted to serve. Thus, an attempt is made to match the appropriate deacons with the appropriate teams. When deacons serve in an area they feel spiritually gifted or passionate about, they tend to enjoy it, do it well, and stick with it. Some examples of gift-based teams might include a hospital visitation team, crisis intervention team, guest follow-up team, shut-in/homebound team, and inactive member team.

Reflect on the Following Questions

> Are our deacons organized for effective ministry? If so, how so? If not, why not?

> If not, which of the above organizational plans might work best in our church?

> What are the greatest barriers to effectiveness in our current deacon plan?

> What are the strengths of our current deacon ministry plan?

> What steps do we need to take to move toward greater organization, intentionality, and effectiveness as a deacon body?

As You Reflect on the Role of Deacons as Described in Scripture, Reflect on the Following Questions

> Is the role of the deacon in our church consistent with the teaching of Scripture?

> If not, how does our current perceived role differ from what is taught in Scripture?

> Do church members view our deacons as true servants? If not, how do they view the deacons?

CHAPTER 3

Deacon Selection

Andy McDonald

Now that we have outlined the biblical qualifications for a deacon and described the role of a deacon in the church, we turn our attention to a practical question: How does a church select their deacons? In this chapter, we will examine five biblical application steps from Acts 6 to help guide a church in the deacon selection process. We will look at the deacon nomination process options and conclude by offering three sample church deacon selection options.

Deacon Selection Process

While there is no clear biblical teaching given for selecting deacons, we can glean some important practical insight from Acts 6 to help guide the process.

In those days, as the disciples were increasing in number, there arose a complaint by the Hellenistic Jews against

the Hebraic Jews that their widows were being over-
looked in the daily distribution. (Acts 6:1 CSB)

In this passage we find the church in a season of growth.
As is often the case during periods of significant expansion,
growing pains emerge. In this case, a complaint arose when one
group of church members felt slighted by another. Complaints
unaddressed often turn into conflict, and unaddressed conflict
can threaten the unity of the body. The problem had gotten
the attention of the Twelve (the apostles) who called the church
together:

> The Twelve summoned the whole company of the dis-
> ciples and said, "It would not be right for us to give up
> preaching the word of God to wait on tables. Brothers
> and sisters, select from among you seven men of good
> reputation, full of the Spirit and wisdom, whom we can
> appoint to this duty. But we will devote ourselves to
> prayer and to the ministry of the word." This proposal
> pleased the whole company. So they chose Stephen,
> a man full of faith and the Holy Spirit, and Philip,
> Prochorus, Nicanor, Timon, Parmenas, and Nicolaus, a
> convert from Antioch. They had them stand before the
> apostles, who prayed and laid their hands on them.
>
> So the word of God spread, the disciples in Jerusalem
> increased greatly in number, and a large group of priests
> became obedient to the faith. (Acts 6:2–7 CSB)

During the meeting, the Twelve expressed both the priority
of fulfilling their own ministry roles and the need to identify and

raise up godly leaders to attend to other important functions of the church. As a result, a God-ordained solution emerged that solved the problem of neglected widows, put down potential disunity in the body, and propelled the church to even greater growth and gospel impact. And out of the midst of this challenging circumstance, the foundation for the role of deacon was born.

For the purpose of this chapter, let's briefly identify some general and practical steps from Acts 6 that will help guide a church in the process of selecting deacons.

Step 1. Call the church together to pray for the deacon selection process.

The leadership gathered the "whole company of the disciples." While it's not explicitly stated here, it's hard to imagine that the apostles, who devoted themselves to prayer (v. 4), would bring the church together to address a problem without taking time to pray. Regardless, prayer is always an appropriate first step in any church or individual decision.

Step 2. Clearly communicate the qualifications of a deacon.

The apostles described the character of a godly servant leader as "men of good reputation, full of the Spirit and wisdom" (v. 3). These men would be entrusted with resources and money. They needed to be mature and trustworthy. Obviously, 1 Timothy 3:8–13 will be the leading passage in this step.

Step 3. Clearly articulate what the role of a deacon entails.

The apostles clearly identified the need. The church needed men to "wait on tables" (Acts 6:2). The job required servant leaders who were both trustworthy and unafraid to get their hands dirty in the administration of this vital ministry.

Step 4. Provide a way for the congregation to be involved in the deacon selection process.

Members were invited to join the selection process. "Brothers and sisters, select from among you seven men" (v. 3). It's not clear as to what level members were involved in selecting names, but that they were involved seems clear.

Step 5. Publicly set apart these men for their service as deacons.

"They had them stand before the apostles, who prayed and laid their hands on them" (v. 6). In this powerful and sacred moment, these men were set apart to serve the church by the laying on of hands. Both the congregation who selected these men and the apostles who laid hands on them participated in setting these men apart for the work of a deacon.

Deacon Nomination Process Options

Questions must be addressed with any process:

Where do we start?

> Pray! Every leader selection process should start with prayer. Who knows better than the heavenly Father

who is best suited to serve, what our church's real needs are, and who is qualified?

Who can nominate?

The entire congregation

The nominating committee

The deacon body

A deacon selection team

Who screens the nominations?

Self-screening using a personal inventory based on biblical and practical qualifications. (This could be used in conjunction with the following screening groups.)

No one (All nominees who agree to serve are placed on a voting ballot.)

The nominating committee

The deacon body

A deacon selection team

Which deacon candidates are presented before the church for vote/affirmation?

All eligible nominees regardless of the number of deacons needed

All screened and eligible nominees regardless of the number of deacons needed

Only the number of deacon candidates needed who have passed the screening process

Seeking to follow biblical guidelines and best practices will greatly increase the chances that mature and godly leaders will be selected and help avoid hurting those not selected. It will also provide a buffer from the pressure to select those who are not best suited to serve.

Following biblical guidelines and best practices will lead a church to lean on their pastor throughout the process. The pastor's knowledge of potential candidates and guidance will prove invaluable in the deacon selection process.

A church may consider narrowing the final list of deacon candidates presented for approval to equal only the number of positions to be filled. This will decrease the likelihood of hurt feelings and unqualified persons being selected.

Three Church Examples of a Deacon Nomination Process

Deacon Selection Process Example 1: First Baptist Church

1. Only those who meet the biblical and church qualifications for deacon and have agreed to serve if selected will be presented to the church for a vote.

2. Deacons selected will serve a three-year term unless they are completing an unexpired term.

3. The final list of names presented to the church will include ordained deacons, not currently serving, who are still qualified to serve and have agreed to serve if selected.

4. Church members will be given the opportunity to submit names for consideration to serve as deacon. Men whose names are submitted, who have not previously served as deacons, will be evaluated by a deacon selection committee comprised of the pastor and active deacons. Only those who meet biblical qualifications will be considered. Note: Men may not be nominated by members of their family.

5. A list of all ordained deacons not currently serving and those recommended by church members will be submitted to the deacon selection committee for prayerful consideration. Note: The deacon selection committee will be made up of the pastor, deacon chairman, deacon vice-chairman, a deacon at large, and three additional church members.

6. All those being considered for deacon at FBC will be asked to complete a deacon questionnaire and return it to the deacon selection committee for review.

7. The deacon selection committee will bring the final slate of names to the full deacon body for their approval.

8. Once approved by the deacon body, the list of nominees will be presented to the whole church at a regular or special called business meeting for final approval. Church members will vote yes or no for each nominee. A ballot must be signed to be accepted. Only nominees receiving 85 percent approval will be able to serve.

9. Deacons serving for the first time will participate in a churchwide ordination service where each will be ordained.

Deacon Selection Process Example 2: Central Baptist Church

1. An announcement is made to the church body that the process for deacon selection is beginning. The pastor preaches a message to the church about the biblical qualifications of a deacon and the role deacons serve at CBC.

2. Church members are asked to prayerfully consider men who meet the biblical qualifications for serving as a deacon and who set a godly example for others to follow. These include, but are not limited to, regular Bible study, prayer, evangelism, Christian service, church attendance, and stewardship.

3. Church members agree to pray for and help the deacons in their role as servant leaders.

4. The pastor calls the church to join him in a prayer gathering as they begin to consider qualified men to serve.

5. After the prayer gathering, church members have two weeks to provide names for consideration as a deacon.

6. At the end of these two weeks, names nominated for deacon are examined and considered for service by the pastor (staff) and the deacon body. This group will produce a list of qualified nominees.

7. The list of nominees produced by the above process is presented to the entire church for their approval. Approval of a nominee requires a two-thirds affirmative vote of members present at a special called meeting.

8. Newly elected deacons then are part of an ordination council. Each will participate in an ordination/installation service where they will begin to serve as a CBC deacon.

Deacon Selection Process Example 3: East Baptist Church

1. The deacon body shall consist of a sufficient number of deacons to support no more than ten church families per deacon.

2. As the deacon nomination process begins, a letter outlining the basic qualifications for the role of deacon will be mailed to each church family. The letter will include a list of all qualified deacon candidates along with a nomination ballot.

3. Members have two weeks to submit a signed nomination ballot.

4. Each EBC member may submit the number of nominees equal to the number of vacancies to be filled for the selection time frame.

5. A deacon counting team will be selected by the deacon chair. The counting team will tabulate the ballots. The counting team will rank the nominees, presenting a list of qualified deacons equal to the number of open positions.

6. The deacon chairman and/or his designee(s) will contact each name on the list to determine if the nominee is willing to serve. If a nominee is unwilling to serve, the next largest vote getter will be contacted. This process will continue until the full complement of deacons is secured.

7. The deacon chairman will report the results of the selection process to the church.

8. Newly elected deacons will begin their term of service.

9. Newly elected deacons who have not been ordained will participate in a special ordination service.

Conclusion

Deacons provide a biblically crucial role in the spiritual vitality and overall welfare of the church. They can often make or break a pastor's ministry, and they greatly impact the spiritual health and vitality of the churches they serve. Therefore, it is imperative that any deacon selection process be prayerful, biblical, thoughtful, and spiritual. A church would be far better off to have only a few deacons when they are "men of good reputation, full of the Spirit and wisdom" (v. 3) than to have a full complement of deacons where many are not spiritually mature and servant minded.

As you consider your deacon selection process, ask yourself these questions:

1. Is our process for selecting deacons a deeply prayerful one? If not, what would it take to make our process one where prayer is driving our process?

2. Do our members have a clear understanding of the biblical qualifications of a deacon and the role a deacon plays in the church? If not, what steps can a pastor take to ensure the selection process includes time to deepen his people's understanding of the qualifications and role of a deacon?

3. Is our church's deacon selection process relatively simple and easy to communicate to our members? If not, what can we do to simplify the process so that it is both effective and easy to follow?

CHAPTER 4

Deacon Ordination

Dr. Larry J. Purcell

The practice of ordination, laying hands on someone, is an ancient practice found in both the Old and New Testaments.[3] The act of laying hands on someone is identifying and agreeing with their being called by the Lord into His service. A more complete explanation of the deacon requirements, role, and selection was previously presented in chapters 1–3 in this deacon handbook. This section will cover the ordination service and provide examples. You can adopt or adjust any of the examples offered as best suits your church's needs and situation.

> Now in those days, when *the number of* the disciples was multiplying, there arose a complaint against the Hebrews by the Hellenists, because their widows were neglected in the daily distribution. Then the twelve summoned the multitude of the disciples and said, "It is not desirable that we should leave the word of God and serve tables. Therefore, brethren, seek out from among

you seven men of *good* reputation, full of the Holy Spirit and wisdom, whom we may appoint over this business; but we will give ourselves continually to prayer and to the ministry of the word."

And the saying pleased whole multitude. And they chose Stephen, a man full of faith and the Holy Spirit, and Philip, Prochorus, Nicanor, Timon, Parmenas, and Nicolas, a proselyte from Antioch, whom they set before the apostles; and when they had prayed, they laid hands on them.

Then the word of God spread, and the number of the disciples multiplied greatly in Jerusalem, and a great many of the priests were obedient to the faith. (Acts 6:1–7 NKJV)

The passage above identifies a conflict in the early church and a group of servant leaders who were easily identified to settle this conflict. These men who were serving the Lord and His people faithfully were publicly set apart by prayer and the act of laying hands on the seven. We can see in Acts 6:1–7 the act of ordaining should not be taken lightly because of how the Holy Spirit was demonstrating in gifts. Later the apostle Paul would offer a more complete list of requirements for the office of pastor and deacon (see chapter 1).

The timing and type of deacon ordination service you want can offer new opportunities for teaching a church about the role of deacons and leadership. If you have an ordination service during a regular worship service, such as on a Sunday night, this can demand a specific format for the time involved. If a special service is called outside of normal gatherings, having a deacon ordination service during the week, such as a Friday or Saturday night, may provide time for a more formal format. Whatever order and format you choose, this is a special event in the lives of these men and a church.

The examples below are added for you to review and adjust to your specific needs or circumstances.

Deacon Ordination 1

Song

Open with Prayer and Welcome

Introduce the Deacon Candidates (Usually the chairman of deacons or minister)

Song

Charge to the Church (Ordained man who candidate requested with your approval. Ask for a list of three to four men they would like to preach, and you choose one.)

Charge to the Deacons (Ordained deacon who candidate requested with your approval. Ask for a list of three to four deacons they would like to speak and pick one.)

Charge to the Candidate (Pastor does this.)

Laying on of Hands (All ordained men can be called forward to participate or just those on an ordaining council.)

Closing Prayer

Note: The deacon candidate does not speak at this service. A pastor added that when he came to a church and they ordained deacons, they required them to speak during the service, but he shared that nowhere in Scripture is this a requirement. If ordained to the ministry, then they speak. After he explained this to the church, they accepted it, and five introverted men allowed their names to be submitted. He further shared those five deacons are their best visitors to hospitals and nursing homes, but they will not speak in public.

Critical questions of belief or practices can be asked by a team such as the pastor and a deacon. The ordaining council can also meet with them privately to discuss issues of beliefs and practices. Much of this should have already been identified by the leadership and congregation, but having this conversation can provide greater confidence of the deacon's calling and ministry service.

Deacon Ordination 2

Worship music to open the service.

Welcome and Prayer (Pastor)

Introduction (Pastor)

> Congregation has presented the deacon candidates before the body and approved by vote of the

membership for ordination into the office of deacon prior to the official ordination service.

Introduce each of the candidates and invite each to share his testimony of salvation.

Candidates will then sit at the front of the church together.

Prayer led by the pastor.

Sermon: Charge can be presented to the candidates and the church. The texts below are good to set the background and requirements of deacons in the early church. (See also chapter 1–3 of the handbook.)

Acts 6

1 Timothy 3:8–13

Prayer for the Candidates (Laying on of Hands)

Place chairs at the altar and invite candidates to sit in them. The ordained men will line up and pray over each new deacon. The men participating in laying on of hands will then sign the certificates before returning to their seats. This offers the candidate a reminder of those who participated in such a special service.

Invite all ordained men of the ordaining counsel and in the congregation who wish to participate to come forward. Take turns laying hands on the candidates and praying over each man.

Prayer of Dedication for New Deacons (This can be the deacon chair.)

Closing remarks by the pastor and welcome to the new deacons. Invite wives to join their husbands, and church members shake hands to congratulate them.

Deacon Ordination 3

The above outlines are simple and easy to follow by any size church. If you wish to add more steps for a more formal presentation, you can use the example below, asking the group of deacon candidates the following questions after each has shared his testimony. These can all be asked one at a time, and the deacons as a group can affirm each.

Worship music to open the service.

Welcome and Prayer (Pastor)

Introduction (Pastor)

Congregation has presented the deacon candidates before the body and approved by vote of the membership for ordination into the office of deacon prior to the official ordination service.

Introduce each of the candidates and invite each to share his testimony of salvation. Candidates will then sit at the front of the church together.

Questions to be affirmed by the deacons (Deacons should affirm each by saying, "We do.")

Do you believe the Word of God is complete, infallible, and the only rule of faith and practice?

Have you read *The Baptist Faith and Message* (2000), and do you affirm it?

Do you affirm support of this church as a faithful steward with your tithes, time, and talents?

Do you accept the responsibility of the office of deacon with this congregation and promise to faithfully perform all the duties?

Do you promise to promote the unity and purity of this church?

Questions to be affirmed by the congregation:

Do you, the members of this church, acknowledge and receive these brothers as deacons, and do you promise to support them with respect, encouragement, and cooperation as they seek to faithfully serve the Lord and the congregation in the office of deacon? (Members affirm by saying, "We do.")

Prayer led by the pastor.

Sermon: A charge can be presented to the candidates and the church. The texts below are good to set the background and requirements of deacons in the early church. (See also chapters 1–3 of the handbook.)

Acts 6

1 Timothy 3:8–13

Prayer for the Candidates (Laying on of Hands)

Place chairs at the altar and invite candidates to sit. The ordained men will line up and pray over each new deacon. The men participating in laying on of hands will then sign the certificates before returning to their seats. This offers the candidate a reminder of those who participated in such a special service.

Invite all ordained men of ordaining counsel and in the congregation who wish to participate to come forward. Take turns laying hands on and praying over each new deacon candidate.

Prayer of Dedication for New Deacons (This can be the deacon chair.)

Closing remarks by the pastor and welcome to the new deacons. Invite wives to join the men and church members to shake hands to congratulate them.

Questions to be affirmed by the deacons:

> Do you believe the Word of God is complete, infallible, and the only rule of faith and practice?

> Have you read *The Baptist Faith and Message* (2000), and do you affirm it?

> Do you affirm support of this church as a faithful steward with your tithes, time, and talents?

> Do you accept the responsibility of the office of deacon with this congregation and promise to faithfully perform all the duties?

> Do you promise to promote the unity and purity of this church?

Questions to be affirmed by the congregation:

> Do you, the members of this church, acknowledge and receive these brothers as deacons, and do you promise to support them with respect, encouragement, and cooperation as they seek to faithfully serve the Lord and the congregation

in the office of deacon? (Members affirm by saying, "We do.")

Following the congregation's affirmation of the deacons, the men, either sitting in chairs at the front or on their knees at the altar, will have ordained men lay hands on them and pray.

Note: *Manual of Forms* by A. H. Hodge offered some ideas that were adjusted to better fit the deacon manual for the section of questions for deacon and congregation.[4]

CHAPTER 5

The Deacons Meeting

Dr. Larry J. Purcell

We all know that calling a meeting takes planning and preparation because we are asking some of our busiest people to come to another meeting. Patrick Lencioni wrote a book about this issue titled *Death by Meeting*.[5] Meetings are not always boring, and yet when asked to attend another one, that may be your first thought or feeling. Deacons meetings should occur on a regular basis to build a sense of purpose and camaraderie. I have seen many meetings cancelled because they seemed to have no purpose or immediate action. This is not always a bad decision, but sometimes meetings can be a critical time for prayer and fellowship. This can be especially true when the church or the deacons are facing new challenges or decisions. This chapter will seek to challenge you in establishing deacons meetings with a clear agenda and setting a spiritual direction, not just business as usual.

Below are some critical questions to help you plan your next deacons meeting and provide an example of an agenda. These are only examples and not meant to cover all situations. You may need to adjust them for the needs of your specific situation or circumstance for a meeting.

What Type of Meeting Is It?

Deacons meetings can be regularly scheduled meetings with the full deacon body or a special called meeting. The type and purpose of the meeting set the boundaries for the planning and who will need to attend. Participants can best be identified by the purpose of the meeting. So, who needs to be included in the meeting? The full deacon body? Do you have rotating deacons? If so, do you want to invite only the deacons who are currently active? Do you wish to invite deacons who may be retired? This can best be determined by what is being discussed during the meeting. If you have *deacons in training* or persons assisting the deacons, such as *yokefellows*, do you need to invite them? If the meeting is a celebration or a training opportunity, you may want to include deacons' wives. Whatever the purpose of the meeting, all deacons meetings should have a designated time of prayer for the church family, its ministries, and outreach. This continues to set necessary boundaries around the meeting as spiritual. This is essential for all deacons meetings but even more so when discussing sensitive issues or concerns in a church. Setting a time limit encourages attendance to meetings.

It would be good to invite all active, inactive, and retired deacons each year for a time of prayer. Each year provides its own challenges, and taking moments to focus on prayer and sharing as a larger group can be spiritually healthy. This can be a great event to celebrate any wins of the past year or challenges being faced ahead.

Reasons to Invite Pastoral Staff

When you have a regularly scheduled deacons meeting, you may want to have all staff present. This allows them to share any updates or needs of ministries and church families. This encourages a team spirit since such meetings are a time of sharing and praying for one another. It is not an oversight meeting unless it is designated as such.

Ground Rules for a Smooth Meeting

Think through some simple and yet effective ground rules that can assist you in keeping the meeting focused and moving forward. We have all been to meetings where only a few dominate the conversation or change the focus of the meeting. Setting clear and agreed-upon ground rules provides boundaries and focus for participants.

Some examples of ground rules to adopt can be:

Be Attitudes

✓ Be confidential.
✓ Be sensitive.
✓ Be focused.

✓ Be involved.

✓ Be finished.

Be confidential.

Much of the material discussed in a deacons meeting may not be confidential. We do want transparency, but confidentiality is critical to disclose information shared in a deacons meeting at the proper time.

Be sensitive.

We may not all agree on every issue or how someone in the ministry team feels or thinks about an issue. The Bible is specific that "there be no divisions among you, but *that* you be perfectly joined together in the same mind and in the same judgment" (1 Cor. 1:10 NKJV).

Be focused.

Sticking to an agenda helps keep the meeting moving forward, but adding to the list will only extend the meeting. This is not saying a new topic is not important; rather it may be a discussion you should have with the pastor and set on the next agenda. I stress a previous point on setting a time limit to the meetings. If more time is involved because of sensitive discussions, this can be established prior to a meeting or during the meeting.

Be involved.

Too often persons attend a meeting and say nothing. You probably have heard someone complain about a decision that was made. When asked what they said in the meeting, too often they said nothing. You have been identified as a leader, and your thoughts and insights will add value to the meeting and future decisions.

Be finished.

Do not leave a meeting with unaddressed anger or frustration.

A good practice is having the rules of the meeting posted or placed on the agenda for a meeting. It is also a good practice to review them before a meeting as you open with prayer.

Closing Meetings

Opening and closing a meeting will vary as to the purpose of the meeting. Some critical aspects to any meeting are the spiritual nature of our calling and ministry. You may be gathering to discuss issues of the church, but this is ministry. Start and end all meetings with prayer. If you are hearing about a person, family, or ministry need, stop and ask one of the leaders to pray specifically about this issue. If you are having a disagreement now or anticipate that a decision may negatively affect some of the congregation, pray. Pray, pray, pray.

Evaluate Meetings

In all areas of life and business, evaluation can be valuable in reflecting on the purpose, the agenda items, and the flow. Did you accomplish the purpose of the meeting? Were all the agenda items addressed? Did new concerns arise during the meeting? Did the meeting flow and close well?

It is always profitable to ask a series of questions as you reflect. It is equally important that you discuss with key leaders attending the meeting to obtain other perspectives. Key leaders will hear from others who may not share with the pastor or chair of the meeting.

Agenda for the Meeting

The below agenda was modified as an example. Dr. Dan Summerlin, senior pastor, Lone Oak First Baptist Church, Paducah, Kentucky, uses this agenda during their regularly scheduled deacons meeting. It can be adopted and adjusted to fit a church or ministry of any size. Regular meetings provide for critical conversations of concerns, needs, issues to be faced, and a time to pray together.

Deacons Meeting Agenda

- Welcome and Prayer
- Financial Report (Go over the month's finances. Our executive pastor or treasurer does this.)
- Pastor's Report (Go over the spiritual issues of the church, review the last month, look at the upcoming calendar events, and talk about future issues. This can be a good time to hear from other staff ministers if they are invited.)

- Administrative Report (Building issues and financial issues are discussed by our executive pastor.)
- Prayer Concerns
- Conclusion

Note from Dr. Summerlin: If I do the pastor's report first, it lays the spiritual foundation for the administrative report.

You see that the agenda provided by Dr. Summerlin is simple and focused. Since it is the regularly scheduled meeting and not a special called one, it provides a clear direction for those in attendance. A clear agenda like this can encourage attendance because it communicates timeliness. If including the staff, they could share what they are doing in their ministry. Such meetings are not meant to be administrative oversight; rather it is a time of sharing and prayer.

Sharing prayer concerns allows the deacons time to tell about their involvement in ministry since the last meeting, such as what families they have called or visited or hospital visits they conducted. Prayer can follow this as needs of the congregation, ministries, and leaders are shared. This presents a shared ministry environment among ministry leaders.

CHAPTER 6

The Relationship between the Pastor and the Deacons

Dr. Paul R. Badgett

So the word of God spread, the disciples in Jerusalem increased greatly in number, and a large group of priests became obedient to the faith. (Acts 6:7 CSB)

It has often been said, "Christianity is not a religion; Christianity is a relationship." This, of course, is a reference to the relationship disciples are to have with God and the relationship they are to have with one another. One would be hard pressed to find a believer who denied the importance of relationships within the body of Christ. Acts 6:7 points out the importance of these relationships. As a result of the relationships that existed between the twelve apostles and the seven selected men of the Spirit, "the word of God spread, the disciples in Jerusalem increased greatly, . . . and a large group of priests became obedient to the faith" (Acts 6:7 CSB).

The pastor and his deacons are to have proper relationships with one another. They are to be of "one heart and mind" (Acts 4:32 csb). Community (fellowship) should exist between the two of them. The Greek word is *koinonia*, which refers to having something in common, "a common problem (sin), a common need (forgiveness), a common hope (Jesus), and a common life (as followers of Jesus)."[6]

So, how are these relationships manifested within the church body? Very simply, pastors need help! It is so easy to become overwhelmed as a pastor. Any pastor could spend most of his time looking out for the physical needs of the church, which only results in neglecting the church's spiritual needs. According to Acts 6, the pastor has two top priorities: prayer and preaching. In short, the deacon is to have a humble servant's heart with the attitude of "Pastor, I'll take care of that while you spend time in prayer" or "Pastor, let me do that while you spend time in the Word." Deacons need to find the need and then seize the opportunity to serve. The needs might be as follows:

- Empty the trash after a church dinner.
- Take food to a widow in need.
- Mow the church lawn.
- Visit members in the hospital.

In addition to meeting the physical needs of the church, the deacon needs to be a friend to the pastor. Pastors can be lonely at times. Too many pastors can identify with the psalmist David, who wrote, "No man cared for my soul" (Ps. 142:4 kjv). It would be wonderful if pastors could say along with John Bisagno, "My best friends are deacons."[7] As best friends, the pastor supports his deacons, and his deacons support him. As a true friend, the deacon may have to correct the pastor, and at other times the pastor may have to correct the deacon. The Bible says, "Faithful are the wounds of a friend" (Prov. 27:6 KJV). When a deacon is a friend to the pastor, he can protect him from making a mistake that would otherwise hurt his ministry. In like manner, when the pastor is a friend to the deacon, he can prevent him from making a mistake that would otherwise hurt his ministry. The Bible says, "A friend loves at all times" (Prov. 17:17 CSB). The deacon should always be a true friend to his pastor.

To build strong relationships, remember birthdays and anniversaries, give honor when honor is due, express appreciation, and offer prayers on a regular basis. This, of course, is advice for the pastor as well as for the deacons. However, the focus here is on deacon ministry. Therefore, for the deacon who wants to build a strong relationship with his pastor, consider the following list:

- Remember the pastor's birthday; send a card.
- Remember the pastor's anniversary; send a note to the pastor's wife.
- Remember to offer the pastor special recognition. For example, honor him before the congregation when he completes his next academic degree.
- Lead the congregation in remembering Pastor Appreciation Sunday.
- Consider the pastor's pay. The Bible says, "The elders who are good leaders are to be considered worthy of double honor, especially those who work

hard at preaching and teaching. For the Scripture says: **Do not muzzle an ox while it is treading the grain**, and 'The worker is worthy of his wages'" (1 Tim. 5:17–18 CSB, emphasis in original text).

- Recognize milestones. Recognize the pastor who has been at the church for a certain number of years. For example, recognize the pastor who has labored at the church in intervals of five, ten, fifteen, twenty, and twenty-five years, and so on.

- Protect the pastor. The Bible says, "Do not receive an accusation against an elder [pastor] except from two or three witnesses" (1 Tim. 5:19 NKJV).

- Include the pastor and his family in your prayers. The Bible says, "First of all, then, I urge that petitions, prayers, intercessions, and thanksgivings be made for everyone . . . [especially] all those who are in authority" (1 Tim. 2:1–2 CSB).

- Protect the pastor from criticism. Speak positive words in the presence of others concerning your pastor.

- When appropriate, express support for the pastor's staff.

Warren Wiersbe is famous for his "Be" books. For example, his "Be" book for the pastoral epistles is titled *Be Faithful*. The chapter dealing with deacons is titled "Follow the Leaders." In keeping with the Wiersbe term "Be," consider the following list, not from Wiersbe, as you consider the deacon-pastor relationship:

- Be a soul winner. Be equipped to tell others about Christ. Take a course in sharing your faith with others. Join your pastor in reaching the lost for Christ.
- Be faithful to your church's visitation program. Support your pastor by setting an example for the rest of the church family as it relates to outreach.
- Be prayerful. Pray for revival in the church and a great awakening in the community. Pray that your pastor's work in the Lord will not be in vain (1 Cor. 15:58).
- Be winsome. Reach out to visitors. Join your pastor in illustrating how much you care about others. Remember, the church is in the people business.
- Be cheerful. Your attitude may well determine the attitude of your church. Your attitude should be good medicine for your pastor (Prov. 17:22a).
- Be willing to change. You should never change the message (Gal. 1:8); you should never change the man (Acts 4:12); however, sometimes you should change the methods. Never say, in the presence of your pastor, the last eight words of a dying church, "We have never done it that way before."
- You have an adversary. The devil can use deacons to cause disharmony as well harmony. Sometimes the devil can use deacons to run the pastor off. Pastors are hurt most by deacon disloyalty and betrayal.
- Be a peacemaker. Help the pastor with conflict. The seven chosen to serve the first-century church were chosen to help the pastors with complaints.

Someone translated Acts 6:3 as follows: "Find seven men you can appoint over this mess!" Sometimes the deacons can build a relationship with the pastor by helping him with a mess.

Seven statements will stagnate your relationship with the pastor. Those statements are as follows:

1. "We have never done it that way before, pastor."
2. "I don't think we are ready for that."
3. "I think we are doing okay with the way things are now."
4. "I don't think we can afford it."
5. "I don't think that is our job."
6. "That may work where you are from, but that will never work here."

Make a list of ways you can help build a good relationship with your pastor. Use the following as an example:

I will pray for my pastor and his family.	Obeying God's Word will bring about a blessing. To fail to pray for the pastor is to forget 1 Timothy 2:1–2.
I will be alert to the enemy's devices.	I would never want to be disloyal to my pastor. The worst kind of hurt for a pastor is disloyalty.
I will be a peacemaker.	I will build relationships with my pastor by helping him with conflict.

In building good relationships, consider the seven steps offered by Les and Leslie Parrott. Those steps are as follows:

- Be a deacon who listens. Try to understand what your pastor is saying.
- Be a deacon who is safe. Be someone your pastor can trust.
- Be a deacon who lends a hand. Help your pastor because you want to and not because you are a deacon.
- Be a deacon who can walk in your pastor's shoes. Learn to see your church through the eyes of your pastor.
- Be a deacon who can receive. In a healthy relationship people meet one another's needs. You should never allow the relationship to become one-sided.
- Be a deacon who can weather turbulence. All relationships will have rough spots. Be mature enough to persevere in a relationship with your pastor.
- Be a deacon who knows when to call it quits. Some relationships are just not going to work. If you find yourself in an unhealthy relationship with your pastor, consider resigning your position as a deacon.

On building good relationships, Les and Leslie Parrot write:

A pioneering band of researchers has recently studied the age-old mystery of what makes people happy, and their answer is not what might be expected. What comes up consistently at the top of the charts is not success, good looks, or any of those enviable assets. The clear winner is relationships—close relationships.[8]

The pastor and his deacons ought to be winners by establishing close relationships. The Bible says, "Two are better than one because they have a good reward for their efforts. For if either falls, his companion can lift him up; but pity the one who falls without another to lift him up" (Eccles. 4:9–10 CSB).

CHAPTER 7

Deacon How-tos

Rick Howerton

Sharing the Gospel

Biblical Foundations

> And Jesus came and spoke to them, saying, "All authority has been given to Me in heaven and on earth. Go therefore and make disciples of all the nations, baptizing them in the name of the Father and of the Son and of the Holy Spirit, teaching them to observe all things that I have commanded you; and lo, I am with you always, even to the end of the age." Amen. (Matt. 28:18–20 NKJV)

> How then shall they call on Him in whom they have not believed? And how shall they believe in Him of whom they have not heard? And how shall they hear without a preacher? (Rom. 10:14 NKJV)

And He said to them, "Go into all the world and preach the gospel to every creature. He who believes and is baptized will be saved; but he who does not believe will be condemned. (Mark 16:15–16 NKJV)

But you shall receive power when the Holy Spirit has come upon you; and you shall be witnesses to Me in Jerusalem, and in all Judea and Samaria, and to the end of the earth." (Acts 1:8 NKJV)

Now then, we are ambassadors for Christ, as though God were pleading through us: we implore you on Christ's behalf, be reconciled to God. (2 Cor. 5:20 NKJV)

The Goal

Lead a gospel conversation so that the unbeliever understands the gospel and is given the opportunity to become a Christ follower.

The Actions

Leading a gospel conversation does not have to be difficult. In His great wisdom, God made the pathway to the cross, forgiveness, and salvation simple. When making the gospel known, verbalize the four steps to salvation.

Step 1: Tell them of God's love for them and of His plan for everyone who receives His offer of grace. Tell them that the Bible says, "For God so loved the world that He gave His only begotten Son, that whoever believes in Him should not perish but have everlasting life" (John 3:16 NKJV). He has a plan for them and longs for them to accept His plan and know Him.

Step 2: Reveal the problem: separation from God. Tell them that sin is what separates us from God. Let them know that because we are human, we are unable to live sinless lives. The Bible says, "For all have sinned and fall short of the glory of God" (Rom. 3:23 NKJV). Help them understand that we are sinful and that "the wages of sin *is* death, but the gift of God *is* eternal life in Christ Jesus our Lord" (Rom. 6:23 NKJV).

Step 3: Make them aware of the cross, God's cure for our sinful lives. Tell them that Christianity is about what Jesus has done for us that we couldn't do for ourselves. He died on the cross to pay for all the sins we ever committed or will ever commit. If we believe in Him and accept His free offer of grace, He forgives us, cleanses us, and accepts us into heaven when we die. Tell them that Jesus did what needed to be done on our behalf. The Bible says, "Who Himself bore our sins in His own body on the tree, that we, having died to sins, might live for righteousness— by whose stripes you were healed" (1 Pet. 2:24 NKJV).

Step 4: Let them know that they must receive Christ to be saved. To cross the bridge and become a Christ follower, they must believe He is the Son of God raised from the dead. The Bible says, "If you confess with your mouth the Lord Jesus and believe in your heart that God has raised Him from the dead, you will be saved" (Rom. 10:9 NKJV).

To become a Christ follower each person must:

- Admit that he is a sinner.
- Ask to be forgiven and turn away from his sins.

- Believe that Jesus died on the cross and was raised from the dead.
- Receive Christ and welcome Him into their heart and strive to live for Him.

If the person you're sharing the gospel with believes the truth and is willing to receive Christ, ask him to repeat the following prayer with you.

God, I realize I'm a sinner in need of a Savior. I believe Jesus rose from the dead. I believe, through His death on the cross, all of my sins will be forgiven. I accept Jesus as my Lord and Savior. From this day forward I will live my life for Him. Thank You for forgiving me, saving me, and for giving me eternal life. Amen.

Encouraging the Pastor

Biblical Foundations

Remember those who rule over you, who have spoken the word of God to you, whose faith follow, considering the outcome of *their* conduct. (Heb. 13:7 NKJV)

Obey those who rule over you, and be submissive, for they watch out for your souls, as those who must give account. Let them do so with joy and not with grief, for that would be unprofitable for you. (Heb. 13:17 NKJV)

Let the elders who rule well be counted worthy of double honor, especially those who labor in the word and doctrine. For the Scripture says, "You shall not muzzle an ox while it treads out the grain," and, "The laborer *is* worthy of his wages." (1 Tim. 5:17–18 NKJV)

Therefore encourage one another and build each other up, just as in fact you are doing. (1 Thess. 5:11 NIV)

And let us consider how we may spur one another on toward love and good deeds, not giving up meeting together, as some are in the habit of doing, but encouraging one another—and all the more as you see the Day approaching. (Heb. 10:24–25 NIV)

Do not let any unwholesome talk come out of your mouths, but only what is helpful for building others up according to their needs, that it may benefit those who listen. (Eph. 4:29 NIV)

The Goal

To build up your pastor so he serves Christ and the church passionately without growing emotionally depleted and physically exhausted.

The Actions

Pastoring is physically and emotionally draining. Pastors carry a load few people in the world do. They are expected to be effective leaders, counselors, administrators, communicators, preachers, community influencers, and biblical scholars. They are responsible for motivating unmotivated people and leading movements. Pastors are to be model Christians and are judged with a level of expectation others are not.

Pastors need and deserve consistent encouragement. Every deacon should make encouraging the pastor a proactive and common practice.

- *Be verbally encouraging.* Few things bring someone's heart to life as much as when a friend they trust looks them in the eyes and tells them how much they mean to them, that they did something effectively, or that they are doing a good job. Someone once wisely said, "Catch people doing something right; then tell them." Don't wait until your pastor has accomplished something of major significance to congratulate or encourage him. Noticing the everyday things and those things others overlook will be most meaningful to your pastor. When possible, verbally encourage your pastor.

- *Be financially encouraging.* First Timothy 5:17–18 (NKJV) reads, "Let the elders who rule well be counted worthy of double honor, especially those who labor in the word and doctrine. For the Scripture says, 'You shall not muzzle an ox while it treads out the grain,' and, 'The laborer *is* worthy of his wages.'" Pastors should be paid in such a way that they can live without the burden of wondering if they can pay their bills. They also deserve an income that makes it possible to occasionally do something special for themselves and/or their families. If the deacons of your church are responsible for determining the pastor's salary and/or benefits, pay the pastor in a way that meets his needs and more. Be sure your pastor receives a Christmas bonus and special gifts on his church service anniversaries. That is when he's served the church for five years, then ten years, then twenty years, and beyond. When possible, passing a gift card to your pastor speaks volumes and is a gift that goes far beyond the card's costs.

- *Be time encouraging.* Effective pastors work many hours. Not only do they work a massive amount of time weekly, but most are also viewed by some members of their congregation as being on call twenty-four hours a day. It's not unusual for a pastor to be called to the hospital or into a crisis anytime day or night. Without time away, they will grow emotionally weary and become ineffective preachers, counselors, and leaders. If your deacon body is responsible for determining the amount of vacation time your pastor receives, be generous. If he isn't getting at least three weeks of vacation a year, the deacons should do what is necessary to make that happen. He should receive four weeks of vacation after serving in full-time ministry a predetermined amount of time. And if the church hasn't already made a sabbatical available, the deacons would be wise to spearhead making a sabbatical possible. And finally, when the pastor is taking his day off, the church should be reminded that he isn't available except in the most crucial situations.

- *Be situationally encouraging.* Pastors are leaders. Leaders are forced to make decisions that don't please everyone. There will always be some who disagree with almost every decision made. These disgruntled church members are frequently hostile and verbalize their discontent. In these situations, a great gift a deacon or the deacon body gives their pastor is encouragement. Even if you disagree with the decision that has been made, thank the pastor for making the best call he knew to make. Stand by him and stand up for him when others speak poorly of him or verbally abuse him.

Making a Hospital Visit

Biblical Foundations

"I *was* naked and you clothed Me; I was sick and you visited Me; I was in prison and you came to Me." (Matt. 25:36 NKJV)

Bear one another's burdens, and so fulfill the law of Christ. (Gal. 6:2 NKJV)

Be kindly affectionate to one another with brotherly love, in honor giving preference to one another; not lagging in diligence, fervent in spirit, serving the Lord; rejoicing in hope, patient in tribulation, continuing steadfastly in prayer; distributing to the needs of the saints, given to hospitality. (Rom. 12:10–13 NKJV)

We then who are strong ought to bear with the scruples of the weak, and not to please ourselves. Let each of us please *his* neighbor for *his* good, leading to edification. (Rom.15:1–2 NKJV)

The Goal

To encourage and inspire the sick while reminding them that the body of Christ is praying for and cares about them. Suppose the person being visited is not saved. In that case, the goal is to encourage them and share the gospel, allowing them to consider becoming a Christ follower.

The Actions

Visiting the sick while they are in the hospital is a unique ministry. Meeting people in their time of deepest physical concern is to meet them when they need encouragement deeply. Hospital visits must be carried out with the primary concern being for the patient and the patient's spiritual needs, while at the same time being careful to adhere to hospital protocols.

Preparing to Visit

In preparation for your visit, pray for the people you will be visiting and that God will make you an agent of His love. Find out when the patient is in treatment. Plan around the patient's treatment schedule. Also, check to see when visiting hours are, and make your visit during those times.

During the Visit

While at the hospital, if the patient's curtain is pulled, the door to their room is closed, or there is a sign on the door indicating special treatment is being used, check at the nurse's station before entering. When you know it is all right to enter, knock lightly on the door and wait for a cue from inside the room that it is okay to come into the room.

When arriving in the room, you may find that family members are there. Greet the family members but remember that you have come to minister to the patient. Give your time and attention to the patient, and avoid mingling with family members. If the nurse or doctor enters the room to take care of the patient or speak with the patient and/or the patient's family, be courteous and leave the room.

When speaking with the patient, do your best to position yourself so you and the patient make eye contact. Be an active listener rather than talking much, and avoid telling stories of your past illnesses or the illnesses of others. Most patients long to be heard and need someone to listen to them. Do not sit on the bed. You should also cut your visit short if the patient is eating. Don't wake the patient if they're sleeping or unresponsive.

Instead, leave a note letting them know you came by and that you and the church are praying for them.

THE LENGTH OF THE VISIT

A visit should last about ten minutes. Most often it is best for a visit to be even shorter. If the person you're visiting needs or wants to talk, feel free to stay longer but be careful. You may weaken the patient who needs rest to recover.

THE VISIT AND SPIRITUAL MATTERS

If the person you're visiting is not saved, ask them about their spiritual condition. If you sense they are open to a conversation about spiritual matters, pursue the discussion with hopes of sharing the gospel and asking them to pray to receive Christ. If you realize they are not interested in a spiritual conversation, don't force the issue. God's timing is perfect, and it's obvious if the moment you're with them isn't in His timing.

Before leaving, with the patient's permission, pray for the patient. If you believe the patient is open to it, reading a Scripture passage that brings comfort and hope is also appropriate.

If you're visiting a terminally ill patient who is saved, be sure to speak of heaven and the hope they have in Christ. If the patient is not saved and they're open to the conversation, share the gospel with them and give them an opportunity to receive Christ.

As you leave, thank them for speaking with you and remind them that you and the church will be praying for them.

Visiting Shut-ins

Biblical Foundations

"'For I was hungry and you gave Me food; I was thirsty and you gave Me drink; I was a stranger and you took Me in; I *was* naked and you clothed Me; I was sick and you visited Me; I was in prison and you came to Me.'

"'Then the righteous will answer Him, saying, 'Lord, when did we see You hungry and feed *You,* or thirsty and give *You* drink? When did we see You a stranger and take *You* in, or naked and clothe *You*? Or when did we see You sick, or in prison, and come to You?' And the King will answer and say to them, 'Assuredly, I say to you, inasmuch as you did *it* to one of the least of these My brethren, you did *it* to Me.'" (Matt. 25:35–40 NKJV)

Let nothing *be done* through selfish ambition or conceit, but in lowliness of mind let each esteem others better than himself. Let each of you look out not only for his own interests, but also for the interests of others. (Phil. 2:3–4 NKJV)

For you, brethren, have been called to liberty; only do not *use* liberty as an opportunity for the flesh, but through love serve one another. (Gal. 5:13 NKJV)

Bear one another's burdens, and so fulfill the law of Christ. (Gal. 6:2 NKJV)

Be kindly affectionate to one another with brotherly love, in honor giving preference to one another; not lagging in diligence, fervent in spirit, serving the Lord; rejoicing in hope, patient in tribulation, continuing steadfastly in prayer; distributing to the needs of the saints, given to hospitality. (Rom. 12:10–13 NKJV)

The Goal

To encourage and inspire the weak while reminding them that the body of Christ is praying for and cares about them. If the person being visited is not saved, the goal is to encourage them and share the gospel with them, allowing them to consider becoming a Christ follower.

The Actions

Visiting with those who are homebound is Christlike and a great encouragement to the precious saints who are brothers and sisters in Christ. Representing Jesus's love through action is the call of a deacon and is a fulfilling obligation. Deacons who make visits of this nature a priority will be incredibly blessed.

Because this is such an important time for the homebound person, a deacon should make the experience as meaningful as possible. The guidance listed below will make that possible.

BEFORE THE VISIT

Before visiting, do two things: pray, and call to set up a time for your visit. Pray that God will allow your words to bring comfort, hope, and help. Pray that God will speak through you and that you will have a heart of love and compassion for the person you're visiting. Also, be sure to call and set up a time to come by. Many people are embarrassed if they haven't had the opportunity to clean the house prior to a guest's arriving. Some homebound people have a strict daily routine they follow as someone cleans for them at a predetermined time each week. They may be involved in scheduled treatment or therapy or have unusual sleep patterns. Calling to make an appointment is essential.

When you call, tell the person you are a deacon at the church and want to come see them and spend a few minutes with them. Be sure not to say things like "I've been assigned to you," or "You're on my list to visit." Statements like these insinuate that you are visiting out of obligation. You want them to realize through action that you care about them and want to show them the love of Christ.

When you are setting up the appointment time, the person may suggest that they don't want you to go to any trouble. Graciously let them know that you want to come by and then suggest a time and day you'd like to come. This should lead to a conversation that will conclude with a date and time on both of your calendars.

Finally, be sure to get something from the church that you can give the homebound person. You'll present this item to them during your visit. A church bulletin, a CD or DVD of Sunday's sermon, a devotional guide, or a note from the church's pastor or the staff member assigned to senior adults is appropriate and welcomed.

WHILE VISITING

Ring the doorbell and/or knock loudly on the door. The person you're visiting may have difficulty hearing. If they don't come to the door quickly, it may be that they didn't hear the doorbell or your knocking. The deacon may believe no one is home and leave without making the visit. Few things are more disappointing to a homebound person than anticipating the deacon visit and believing the deacon didn't come as promised.

Allow the person you're visiting to serve you if requested. For instance, if the individual asks if they can get you coffee or a slice of pie, graciously accept the offer. This may be one of the few times the individual can serve others.

Be an active listener. Many homebound people are alone much of the time. When others are with them, people come in groups and speak around the homebound person. If they come individually, many will just sit with them without conversing with them. A listening ear and a conversation are cherished gifts. To start the conversation ask, "What's been going on with you?," or "What have you been thinking about lately?" A surefire way to start a conversation with most people in this situation is to say, "Tell me about your family." During the conversation, be sure to tell them what's going on at the church. Telling them what is happening at church connects them with the church body and inspires them. If they are continuing to give to the church, remind them that their giving is making a difference.

Give them something from the church. Bringing something from the church they can keep by their side is a constant reminder that they are not forgotten. As mentioned, good options include a church bulletin, a CD or DVD of Sunday's sermon, a devotional guide, or a note from the church's pastor or the staff member assigned to senior adults.

Administer the Lord's Supper (optional). Some traditions allow and suggest deacons administer the Lord's Supper while making visits to the homebound. Below is an easy step-by-step guide that will be helpful.

1. Pray, asking God to bless the time of reflection and celebration.

2. Read 1 Corinthians 11:23–24, "For I received from the Lord that which I also delivered to you: that the Lord Jesus on the *same* night in which He was betrayed took bread; and when He had given thanks, He broke *it* and said, 'Take, eat; this is My body which is broken for you; do this in remembrance of Me'" (NKJV).

3. Keep a piece of the bread while giving the bread to the homebound person and partake of the bread together.

4. Read 1 Corinthians 11:25, "In the same manner *He* also *took* the cup after supper, saying, 'This cup is the new covenant in My blood. This do, as often as you drink *it*, in remembrance of Me'" (NKJV).

5. Keep a cup of juice for yourself and partake of the cup together.

6. Read 1 Corinthians 11:26, "For as often as you eat this bread and drink this cup, you proclaim the Lord's death till He comes" (NKJV).

7. Close by praying and/or singing a hymn together.

Before leaving be sure to do the following:

- Tell them they are missed, but do not make it sound like the church is upset they're not attending.
- Read a Scripture passage of hope and comfort. Psalm 23 is an excellent choice.
- Pray for the person you're visiting.

Close by:

- Reminding them that the church cares about them and is praying for them.
- Asking them if there's anything the church can do for them. Be careful not to make any promises, and involve others to meet the person's needs if necessary.
- Thanking them for allowing you to come.
- Letting them know that visiting with them was an inspiration to you. Everyone needs to know they're making a difference in the lives of others. This momentary word of encouragement will mean much to the homebound person you're visiting.

When There's a Death

Biblical Foundations

Bear one another's burdens, and so fulfill the law of Christ. (Gal. 6:2 NKJV)

And if one member suffers, all the members suffer with *it;* or if one member is honored, all the members rejoice with *it.* (1 Cor. 12:26 NKJV)

Blessed *be* the God and Father of our Lord Jesus Christ, the Father of mercies and God of all comfort, who comforts us in all our tribulation, that we may be able to comfort those who are in any trouble, with the comfort with which we ourselves are comforted by God. (2 Cor. 1:3–4 NKJV)

Therefore, my beloved brethren, be steadfast, immovable, always abounding in the work of the Lord, knowing that your labor is not in vain in the Lord. (1 Cor. 15:58 NKJV)

The Goal

Partner with others to meet the grieving person's emotional and physical needs while reminding them of the hope we have in Christ.

The Actions

Deacons are sometimes called on when there's a death in the church. In these situations, each church uses deacons differently. Check with your pastor to see what role the deacons carry out when there's a death in the church family.

PRACTICAL NEEDS

When a household experiences the loss of a loved one, any of the following may require the deacon body's attention. Taking care of these needs or assigning them to ministry teams will significantly help the hurting family and allow them to give their full attention to grief and other timely matters.

- Call family members and close friends to make them aware of the death.
- Clean the home of the deceased. This is especially important as family members will be coming in from out of town for the funeral.
- Purchase groceries, toilet paper, etc. This is important as family members will be arriving at the home of the grief-stricken individual.
- Bring meals to the household of the deceased. In many instances, family members come from out of town days before the funeral. Taking care of at least two meals a day is an excellent service to the family.
- Drive children to and from school and other events.
- Mow the lawn.
- Assist with thank-you notes.
- Organize a meal to be served to family members following the funeral service.
- Ask the grieving how you and/or the church might assist them. Don't make promises, but, when possible, meet the needs of those who are grieving.

Deacons are often called upon to visit with those who have lost loved ones. Sometimes deacons are the first to connect with and show care for a grieving church member.

Use the following practices:

- The ministry of presence. The grieving person's greatest need is to be heard. But in some instances they aren't talkative. Your being in the room for a while may be the most important need you meet.
- Be an active listener. An active listener listens more than he talks, keeps eye contact throughout the conversation, and has as his goal to allow the grieving family member the opportunity to be heard.
- Don't force the grieving to talk or offer advice about how to grieve.
- Don't interrupt the grieving family member as they are speaking. They need to be heard and allowed to speak openly about their feelings. They may voice regrets, anger, disappointment, or their discontent with God. Allow these types of statements without contradicting or questioning the truthfulness of their comments.
- Don't tell stories of your own loss or something that has happened to you. The person you're with needs to be listened to, not forced into listening mode.
- Let the grieving family member know that you realize the significance of their loss.

- Once the individual has been allowed to speak openly, thank them for sharing their feelings and share a personal memory you have of the deceased. By doing so, you open the door for others in the room to share stories. This brings healing and aids in moving family members of the deceased into the grief process.
- Before leaving the home or funeral home, pray with everyone present. If the entire family is present, get their attention and ask permission to pray for them. Remind them that the pastor/pastors and the church love them and are praying for them.
- If it seems appropriate (if the family is made up of unbelievers, many of the verses won't be appropriate), use any of the Scripture verses below to encourage the family. Read one of these passages before praying with/for the family. Do not read more than one passage unless you feel compelled to do so by the Holy Spirit or the family requests it.

But I do not want you to be ignorant, brethren, concerning those who have fallen asleep, lest you sorrow as others who have no hope. For if we believe that Jesus died and rose again, even so God will bring with Him those who sleep in Jesus.

For this we say to you by the word of the Lord, that we who are alive *and* remain until the coming of the Lord will by no means precede those who are asleep. For the Lord Himself will descend from heaven with a shout, with the voice of an archangel, and with the trumpet of God. And the dead in Christ will rise first. Then we who are alive *and* remain shall be caught up together with them in the clouds to meet the Lord in the air. And thus we shall always be with the Lord. Therefore comfort one another with these words. (1 Thess. 4:13–18 NKJV)

The LORD *is* my shepherd;
I shall not want.
He makes me to lie down in green pastures;
He leads me beside the still waters.
He restores my soul;
He leads me in the paths of righteousness
For His name's sake.
Yea, though I walk through the valley of the shadow of
    death,
I will fear no evil;
For You *are* with me;
Your rod and Your staff, they comfort me.
You prepare a table before me in the presence of my
    enemies;
You anoint my head with oil;
My cup runs over.
Surely goodness and mercy shall follow me
All the days of my life;
And I will dwell in the house of the LORD
Forever. (Ps. 23 NKJV)

Weeping may endure for a night,
But joy *comes* in the morning. (Ps. 30:5 NKJV)

To everything *there is* a season,
A time for every purpose under heaven:
A time to be born,
And a time to die;
A time to plant,
And a time to pluck *what is* planted;
A time to kill,
And a time to heal;
A time to break down,
And a time to build up;
A time to weep,
And a time to laugh;
A time to mourn,
And a time to dance. (Eccles. 3:1–4 NKJV)

The waters of the first conversation and conversations that follow must be carefully waded through. Saying the wrong thing can have devastating consequences.

DON'T SAY

Many of the following statements are theologically incorrect. All of them are inappropriate and hinder the goal of comforting the grieving.

- "I know how you feel."
- "Things could be worse. I know someone who . . ."
- "It will get easier."

- "There is a reason for everything. In time you'll understand why this was in God's will."
- "He/she is in a better place."
- "You need to be strong for everyone. There will be time to cry later."
- "God never gives us more than we can handle."
- "It was his/her time to go."
- "God needed him/her in heaven."
- "You can remarry."
- "You can have more children."

The Deacon and Prayer

Biblical Foundations

Confess *your* trespasses to one another, and pray for one another, that you may be healed. The effective, fervent prayer of a righteous man avails much. (James 5:16 NKJV)

Therefore I exhort first of all that supplications, prayers, intercessions, *and* giving of thanks be made for all men. (1 Tim. 2:1 NKJV)

For this reason we also, since the day we heard it, do not cease to pray for you, and to ask that you may be filled with the knowledge of His will in all wisdom and spiritual understanding; that you may walk worthy of the Lord, fully pleasing *Him,* being fruitful in every good work and increasing in the knowledge of God; strengthened with all might, according to His glorious power, for all patience and longsuffering with joy; giving thanks to the Father who has qualified us to be partakers of the inheritance of the saints in the light. (Col. 1:9–12 NKJV)

Praying always with all prayer and supplication in the Spirit, being watchful to this end with all perseverance and supplication for all the saints—and for me, that utterance may be given to me, that I may open my mouth boldly to make known the mystery of the gospel, for which I am an ambassador in chains; that in it I may speak boldly, as I ought to speak. (Eph. 6:18–20 NKJV)

Is anyone among you sick? He should call for the elders of the church, and they are to pray over him, anointing him with oil in the name of the Lord. The prayer of faith will save the sick person, and the Lord will raise him up; if he has committed sins, he will be forgiven. Therefore, confess your sins to one another and pray for one another, so that you may be healed. The prayer of a righteous person is very powerful in its effect. (James 5:14–16 CSB)

The Goal

For the church to know the love of the deacon body and for the church to experience the power of God.

The Actions

Deacons are the church's front line. In many churches, they hear the needs of and are responsible for the care of the church body. While meeting physical needs is a great gift to the church membership, praying for them from a heart of love exceeds all other actions. God's intervention in His people's lives elevates Him and creates an environment of celebration and joy.

Deacons should pray personally for the church body and be able to lead prayer gatherings.

PERSONAL PRAYER

Personal prayer times are significant and essential times. In these times alone with God, every deacon can purify his heart before God and pray passionately and unhindered for church members. The times of personal prayer should include the following prayers.

PERSONAL REPENTANCE

David wrote, "If I had cherished sin in my heart, the Lord would not have listened; but God has surely listened and has heard my prayer" (Ps. 66:18–19 NIV). Unconfessed sin housed in an unrepentant heart is an obstacle to effective prayer. At the beginning of the prayer time, a deacon would be wise to confess any unconfessed sin and commit to walking away from that sin or those sins.

PASTOR, STAFF, AND CHURCH LEADERSHIP

The load of church leadership is heavy. The pastor, church staff, and elders are burdened with each congregant's spiritual health, the ministries they oversee, weekly preparation to preach and teach, equipping the church body to do ministry, counseling, conflict resolution, and many other duties.

These church leaders are often called upon to be professionals in areas no one has prepared them for. The prayers of each deacon are essential. When praying for the church leaders, you will want to pray specifically for the following:

- Wisdom and discernment in all matters
- Clearly seeing God's direction
- Protection from the flesh and Satan's attacks
- Protection for their families
- Direction as they prepare to preach and teach
- That they will be consistent in protecting themselves by taking a Sabbath, taking care of their bodies, and exercising
- That they will experience and realize the love of the congregation
- That they will be able to overlook the negative comments or defamatory statements of those who are serially disgruntled

PRAY FOR ONE ANOTHER, DEACONS PRAYING FOR DEACONS

A deacon body is made up of people sharing common responsibilities and mindsets. Each deacon has been blessed with the opportunity to minister to the congregation and has met the same biblical requirements. With these commonalities in play, the group should feel more like a body than a board. A deacon board might be described as a group of businessmen coming together at predetermined times to make decisions and have little spiritual interaction. However, a deacon body is best described as a small group coming together to pray for and strategize to care for the church members. When the board meets, they have business in mind. When a small group gathers, they have the needs of the other group members in mind as well as the needs of others in the congregation.

Every deacon team should see themselves as a deacon body. When they do, praying for one another is intuitive. Some important things to pray for are noted below.

- A consistent daily walk with Christ
- A servant's heart
- Love and honor for the pastor, staff, and elders
- A deep Christlike love for the congregation
- A passion for caring for and meeting the needs of the congregation
- Unity within the deacon body
- Protection from the flesh and Satan's attacks
- Protection for their families

CHURCH MEMBERS

Acts 6:1b tells us why the first deacons were chosen. It reads, "Because their widows were neglected in the daily distribution" (NKJV). Some of the congregation's needs weren't being met. The deaconship was established to meet some of the needs of the congregation.

One of the most essential practices of a deacon is praying for church members. Pray for specific needs as you become aware of them. It's also important for deacons to pray for the following things as they pray for the church body.

- Unity
- Spiritual growth in each individual life
- That members will share the gospel with others
- That they will stand firm in their faith when in the world
- A hunger for God's Word
- A passion to care for the poor and disheartened
- Consistency in worship and group attendance
- That they will give a tithe and beyond
- That they will be shining examples of Jesus's love at school, in their workplaces, and when in recreational settings

Leading a Prayer Meeting

Deacons are often called on to lead a prayer meeting. Whether the meeting is for a large group or for twelve or fewer, the following guide will be helpful. This one-hour model is an excerpt taken from John Franklin's book, *And the Place Was Shaken*.

The one-hour model format consists of five segments: Focus on God, Respond from the Heart, Seek First the Kingdom, Present Your Requests, and Close in Celebration.

Focus on God (10–15 minutes)

The leader must start with God if the rest of the hour is to be God centered. Pray ahead of time and ask God what aspect(s) about Himself He wants you to highlight. Use music, Scripture, or testimony to focus the people on God. The primary purpose of this time is to help hearts get oriented to and prepared to meet God.

Respond from the Heart (10 minutes)

Whenever the people of God truly focus on God, their hearts respond. You need to give your people time to respond to Him. They can do this in any number of ways, including silent prayer, group prayer, and singing, but you are creating the time for the Holy Spirit's work in the heart of His people. The primary purpose of this time is to let the heart of God's people respond to Him.

Seek First the Kingdom (20–25 minutes)

We put His agenda/desires/purposes ahead of our own. In the Lord's Prayer, Jesus concluded by telling us if we seek the kingdom first, God will meet our needs. By creating this as a segment, you build a platform into the prayer meeting to move people to God's agenda. You will pray for the things of God such as the lost, missions, koinonia among believers, the upcoming VBS, and ministry to the homeless. You will exalt the things that edify the church and reach the world. The primary purpose of this time is to help the people of God be on God's agenda.

Present Your Requests (10–15 minutes)

Here you create a segment to pray for the needs and concerns of the people. You will lift up the sick, the hurting, and personal requests. You do this through activities that involve all the people in ministering to one another. The primary purpose of this time is to let people minister to one another by praying for one another.

Close in Celebration (5 minutes)

After spending time in the presence of God, encountering His goodness, casting our burdens on Him, being built up, and having our relationship renewed afresh from His touch, the people of God usually want to respond with thanksgiving and celebration. Some type of closing in which their hearts can praise or thank God is appropriate. Often music will be a good way to do this. The primary purpose of this time is to affirm the blessing of having been in God's presence.[9]

Serving the Lord's Supper

Biblical Foundations

Then He took the cup, and gave thanks, and said, "Take this and divide *it* among yourselves; for I say to you, I will not drink of the fruit of the vine until the kingdom of God comes."

And He took bread, gave thanks and broke *it,* and gave *it* to them, saying, "This is My body which is given for you; do this in remembrance of Me."

Likewise He also *took* the cup after supper, saying, "This cup *is* the new covenant in My blood, which is shed for you. (Luke 22:17–20 NKJV)

For I received from the Lord that which I also delivered to you: that the Lord Jesus on the *same* night in which He was betrayed took bread; and when He had given thanks, He broke *it* and said, "Take, eat; this is My body which is broken for you; do this in remembrance of Me." In the same manner *He* also *took* the cup after supper, saying, "This cup is the new covenant in My blood. This do, as often as you drink *it,* in remembrance of Me."

For as often as you eat this bread and drink this cup, you proclaim the Lord's death till He comes. (1 Cor. 11:23–26 NKJV)

Therefore whoever eats this bread or drinks *this* cup of the Lord in an unworthy manner will be guilty of the body and blood of the Lord. But let a man examine himself, and so let him eat of the bread and drink of the cup. For he who eats and drinks in an unworthy manner eats and drinks judgment to himself, not discerning the Lord's body. (1 Cor. 11:27–29 NKJV)

The Goal

Reverently prepare and deliver the Lord's Supper elements, being certain all is in order after the Lord's Supper service is completed.

The Actions

Deacons are the primary source of delivery of the elements of the Lord's Supper. While all the congregation sees is the delivery of the symbolic body and blood of Christ being doled out by the deacons, the deacons are also responsible for the preparation of and the cleanup after the Lord's Supper has been taken.

An effective deacon body will use three steps when carrying out their role: (1) preparation, (2) delivery, and (3) cleanup. The following procedures are suited to churches passing the elements to the congregation via plates and trays. The three steps will be helpful no matter the Lord's Supper approach.

Preparation

The Lord's Supper cannot be accomplished efficiently without careful preparation. The following procedures will assure these goals are accomplished.

- *Spiritual Preparation.* Each deacon must examine himself before receiving the Lord's Supper (1 Cor. 11:27–29).
- *Attire.* It is best if the attire of the deacons reflects the attire of the church members being served.
- The deacon primarily responsible for the Lord's Supper must determine how many deacons are required and assign roles. The roles will include the preparation of the Lord's Supper elements, the delivery of the Lord's Supper elements, and the cleanup following the Lord's Supper service.
- *Assigning Duties.* Three teams are suggested: (1) preparation team (those who prepare the elements to be served, (2) delivery team (those who serve the Lord's Supper elements to the church members, (3) cleanup team (those who clean up following the Lord's Supper service). In a small to midsize church, most or all of the deacons will engage in all three stages.

DELIVERY

The number of congregants in attendance and the rows to be served will determine the number of plates and trays needed and the number of deacons required to serve.

Step 1. At the appropriate time, deacons move from their typical worship locations to the church's front row.

Step 2. The pastor removes the covers from the stacks of bread plates.

Step 3. Two deacons (most often the chairman and vice-chairman) lift the stack of plates.

Step 4. The plates are carried to the most exterior deacon on the side of the church the deacon chairman or vice-chairman are responsible for. The deacon takes one plate and proceeds to his place of service (the first pew his plate will be passed to).

Step 5. The second deacon from the end of the row will take a plate and proceed to his place of service (the first pew his plate will be passed to). This process continues until all plates are passed out and all deacons are standing next to the row they will be serving.

Step 6. Each deacon serves his assigned section in the same fashion the offering plate is used, with one deacon at the end of each row passing the plate to the row ahead.

Step 7. Once the deacon has distributed the element to every person in his section, he should remain where he is, hold the plate in his hand, and wait for the pastor to make eye contact with him. This is the signal that every person has been served.

Step 8. When alerted, the deacons should return to their original seats on the church's front row and remain standing until the deacon chair or vice-chair relieves them of their trays. Prior to the tray being taken from each deacon, each deacon should take a piece of the bread for himself and remain standing.

Step 9. Once all the trays have been gathered, the deacon chair and vice-chair will reverently return the trays to their original positions on the Lord's Supper table.

Step 10. The pastor will place the lids on the trays and signal for the deacons to be seated.

The same process will be used when delivering the symbolic blood of Jesus (fruit of the vine).

CLEANUP

The following responsibilities must be accomplished following the Lord's Supper.

- Gather Lord's Supper cups and dispose of them.
- Clean plates and trays and return them to their storage locations.

Procuring an Interim Pastor

Biblical Foundations

For this reason I left you in Crete, that you should set in order the things that are lacking, and appoint elders in every city as I commanded you. (Titus 1:5 NKJV)

However, it seemed good to Silas to remain there. Paul and Barnabas also remained in Antioch, teaching and preaching the word of the Lord, with many others also. (Acts 15:34–35 NKJV)

The Goal

To acquire the interim pastor of God's choosing for the betterment of the church and to accomplish predetermined responsibilities.

The Actions

While this isn't the case for every church, an interim pastor is acquired by the deacon body in many churches. The following step-by-step guide will be helpful.

Step 1. Examine the church's constitution and bylaws. Before making any decisions, see what guidelines and expectations are in the church's constitution and bylaws. The binding documents of the church and all expectations found in them must be followed.

Step 2. Determine the role of the interim pastor. One of the following titles and descriptions will be right for your church. Deciding which type of interim a church uses is based on the needs of the church.

> *Transitional pastor.* A transitional pastor is a seasoned church leader capable of guiding a church through a process leading a church to be a healthy church body. He is responsible for providing pastoral leadership,

for aiding the church in clarifying her core values and vision, working with the transition team to deal with all obstacles to church growth and health, providing guidance for the pastor search team, and preparing the church for the arrival of the next pastor.

Pulpit supply. Some churches are blessed with a strong staff team and/or deacon body capable of carrying out many of the church's pastoral duties. Churches blessed with this kind of leadership may hire an interim pastor whose only responsibility is to preach and teach at agreed-upon times.

Interim pastor. A traditional interim pastor is responsible for carrying out many of the church's ongoing pastor's responsibilities. Seldom is an interim pastor accountable for every duty an ongoing pastor does. Some churches require the interim to visit those who are sick, preside over meetings, meet with committees, etc. Before interviewing an interim pastor candidate, the deacons should determine what will be expected of the interim pastor. These expectations should be in written form and discussed with the candidate. The deacon body must allow the interim pastor the opportunity to negotiate which expectations he'll carry out and those he is unable or unwilling to do.

Step 3. Acquire a list of prospective interim/transitional pastor candidates. Speak with denominational leaders at the local and state level, other churches who have recently used an interim/transitional pastor, and ministries specifically designed for aiding churches in finding an interim/transitional pastor. Interim Pastor Ministries is a great option. You can visit www.interim-pastors.com for more information.

Step 4. Determine the interim/transitional pastor's compensation.

Compensation Formula One

The following is a formula based on weekly units instead of weekly hours and/or weekly worship services that assists in calculating the salary portion of an interim pastor's compensation.

1. Each day has three (3) units (morning, afternoon, and evening).

2. Each seven-day week, therefore, has twenty-one (21) units.

3. On an average, a full-time pastor works thirteen–fifteen (13–15) weekly units per week. This assumes the pastor has a day off plus Saturday off each week and is based on five (5) days.

4. Calculate the dollar amount of the total compensation package per weekly unit the church paid its former pastor or amount budgeted for the new pastor, whichever is greater.

(Annual Compensation Package divided by 52 = Weekly Amount)

(Weekly Compensation Amount divided by 13 to 14 Units = Weekly Unit Amount)

5. Determine the number of weekly units the interim pastor will work per week.

- Sundays should be counted as three units if there are one morning and one evening service.
- Sundays should be counted as three units if there are only two morning services.
- If there are two morning services and one evening services for a total of three services, Sunday should be counted as 3.5 units.
- An additional unit should be added if the Interim is available for consultation and/or attends necessary meetings.
- Allow at least two units for preparation and one for travel time (at least three units).
- Consideration for an additional unit should be given if the interim pastor has to stay overnight.

6. Pay the interim pastor the same dollar amount per weekly unit as the church paid its former pastor or the budgeted amount for the new pastor, whichever is greater.

(Weekly Unit Amount multiplied by Number of Weekly Units = Weekly Compensation for Interim Pastor)

Note: Adjustments to this formula and the interim pastor's compensation might have to be made depending on variable circumstances, which include, but are not limited to, the pastor's experience, training, skills, etc.

Protection coverage. A portion of the interim pastor's compensation, at his discretion, may be designated as insurance and/or annuity and/or housing allowance. Such coverage should be agreed upon according to the interim pastor's personal needs, tax status, and current IRS guidelines to best benefit the interim pastor.

Reimbursable expenses. In addition to salary, the church should pay accountable reimbursable expenses (mileage, lodging, etc.). Such expenses should be paid separately from salary and in accordance with current IRS guidelines.

Compensation Formula Two

Another formula used by the North American Mission Board in calculating the interim pastor's compensation is:

1. Pay the interim pastor 60 percent of the greater of the former pastor's total compensation package or of the total compensation package budgeted for the new pastor. (This formula is usually used if the interim pastor is available for Wednesday services.)

2. Pay the interim pastor 50 percent of the greater of the total compensation of the former pastor or of the total compensation budgeted for the new pastor.

3. In making the decision on how to compensate the interim pastor, the following should be considered.

- The units of time he gives the church including preparation, travel, overnight stays, and services preached or led.
- His availability for meeting with staff, deacons, and various leaders of the church.
- His availability to counsel, advise, and give leadership by phone and email.
- His training, experience, and specials skills.
- His value to the church in leading it through a productive interim period and preparing it for the ministry of the new pastor.

(Compensation formulas used by permission, Dr. Stephen C. Rice, church consulting and revitalization team leader, Kentucky Baptist Convention.)

Step 5. Interview the interim/transitional pastor. Clearly define expectations and compensation. Also, be sure to negotiate a covenant agreement with the candidate. The covenant agreement should include expected duties, the compensation agreement, expenses that will be paid, and any other employment conditions.

Step 6. Bring the interim pastor recommendation to the church body for consideration.

Preparing and Delivering a Sermon/Teaching

Biblical Foundations

Preach the word! Be ready in season *and* out of season. Convince, rebuke, exhort, with all longsuffering and teaching. (2 Tim. 4:2 NKJV)

For Christ did not send me to baptize, but to preach the gospel, not with wisdom of words, lest the cross of Christ should be made of no effect. (1 Cor. 1:17 NKJV)

Be diligent to present yourself approved to God, a worker who does not need to be ashamed, rightly dividing the word of truth. (2 Tim. 2:15 NKJV)

And I, brethren, when I came to you, did not come with excellence of speech or of wisdom declaring to you the testimony of God. For I determined not to know anything among you except Jesus Christ and Him crucified. I was with you in weakness, in fear, and in much trembling. And my speech and my preaching *were* not with persuasive words of human wisdom, but in demonstration of the Spirit and of power, that your faith should not be in the wisdom of men but in the power of God. (1 Cor. 2:1–5 NKJV)

The Goal

Prepare and preach an effective, gospel-centered sermon or teaching when called upon.

The Actions

While it is unusual, there will be times when a deacon is called on to preach or teach in the pastor's absence. This may feel like a daunting task, but it need not be. The book *Creative Bible Teaching* by Lawrence O. Richards and Gary J. Bredfeldt provides an easy four-phase sermon that is easy to prepare and deliver. The four-phase sermon includes the following: Hook – Book – Look – Took.[10]

Hook. The hook is an attention-getter that grasps the listener's attention and reveals the direction and purpose of the sermon/teaching. A hook can be in the form of a story, an object lesson, a joke, or any other mode through which the congregation's attention is captured and the primary point of the sermon is revealed.

Book. After grabbing the congregation's attention, it's time to take the people to the Word of God. Book gives proper attention to the narrative of the text. This part of the sermon demands that the preacher spends quality time studying the biblical text and, when preaching, provide some necessary background information. Too many preachers and teachers skip the careful reading of the text and the background of the text and move directly to the explanation of the text.

Look. Look is about the implications of the text. What truths does the text describe to us? What doctrine or truth is made known? Keep in mind that a specific person wrote the text to respond to a particular situation that must be understood first. Then timeless truths are discovered. Knowing first the Bible background and its focus helps guide the proper interpretation and application.

Took. Took is the application phase of the sermon. Application unearths specific ways the listener will seek to apply the truths learned from the text.

Equipping Future Deacons

Biblical Foundations

> And the things that you have heard from me among many witnesses, commit these to faithful men who will be able to teach others also. (2 Tim. 2:2 NKJV)

> As iron sharpens iron,
> So a man sharpens the countenance of his friend. (Prov. 27:17 NKJV)

> Give *instruction* to a wise *man*, and he will be still wiser;
> Teach a just man, and he will increase in learning. (Prov. 9:9 NKJV)

> One generation shall praise Your works to another,
> And shall declare Your mighty acts. (Ps. 145:4)

The Goal

Equip every deacon to serve Jesus's bride effectively.

The Actions

Equipping deacons is an essential task that every deacon body must proactively engage in. The training each deacon needs will vary based on the church's deacon ministry strategy. Each ministry plan—the Deacon Family Ministry Plan, Deacons Ministering through Sunday School Classes, Deacon-Led Ministry Teams, and Gift-Based Deacon Teams—will have its training nuances.

There should be two phases to all deacon training. The first phase is foundational and can be done in a classroom setting. The second phase is relational and must be done on an "as you minister" basis.

Foundational Deacon Training

When a new deacon begins to serve, he needs the following questions to be answered.

- What are the expectations of a deacon as related to our approach to deacon ministry?
- How often and what days and times are the deacons meetings?
- What is the role of every deacon during each deacons meeting?
- How do deacons relate to the pastor and church staff?
- What reports are to be filled out, and what is the system through which a deacon finds and turns them in?
- Who is each deacon accountable to?
- Who is assigned to each deacon to equip them for ministry?
- What guiding documents or books are required reading?
- What is a deacon's responsibility when conflict arises within the deacon body?

- Who will contact each deacon, and how will they be contacted when there is a need to be met?
- What ministry is each deacon responsible for accomplishing unprompted?
- When do deacons prepare and distribute the Lord's Supper elements, and what role does each deacon play?
- What biblical responsibilities is every deacon required to live out—tithing, attending worship weekly, sharing the gospel, being an active member of a Sunday school class or small group, etc.?

Relational

The best deacon training is on-the-job training, a seasoned deacon working with a new deacon. When teaching a skill, the following five-step process is most effective.

- Step 1. I do; you watch.
- Step 2. You do; I watch.
- Step 3. I encourage you for what you did well and share what you need to work on.
- Step 4. You try again and again until you get it right.
- Step 5. I set you free to do that thing on your own.

Responding to Criticism and Slander

Biblical Foundations

"Moreover if your brother sins against you, go and tell him his fault between you and him alone. If he hears you, you have gained your brother. But if he will not hear, take with you one or two more, that 'by the mouth of two or three witnesses every word may be established.' And if he refuses to hear them, tell *it* to the church. But if he refuses even to hear the church, let him be to you like a heathen and a tax collector." (Matt. 18:15–17 NKJV)

Let the word of Christ dwell in you richly in all wisdom, teaching and admonishing one another in psalms and hymns and spiritual songs, singing with grace in your hearts to the Lord. (Col. 3:16 NKJV)

A perverse man sows strife,
And a whisperer separates the best of friends. (Prov. 16:28 NKJV)

He who goes about *as* a talebearer reveals secrets;
Therefore do not associate with one who flatters with his lips. (Prov. 20:19 NKJV)

Hide me from the secret plots of the wicked,
From the rebellion of the workers of iniquity,
Who sharpen their tongue like a sword,

And bend *their bows to shoot* their arrows—bitter words,
That they may shoot in secret at the blameless;
Suddenly they shoot at him and do not fear.
(Ps. 64:2–4 NKJV)

The Goal

Respond to criticism and accusations in a way that diminishes conflict, practicing biblical requirements.

The Actions

Deacons are often approached by church members concerned about the church leadership's decisions, changes being made, a statement made by the pastor when preaching (or in conversation), or hearsay making its way through the gossip mill. Deacons are also asked to address conflicts between members. Sometimes people believe deacons should discipline a church member.

Deacons are the gatekeepers to church unity. The response they give will either aid in bringing peace or promoting division. When a deacon finds himself in conversation with someone in the mindset mentioned, the following practices are essential.

- When approached by a congregant about someone else in the church body, the pastor, or a staff member, encourage the church member to speak directly with the person they're talking about. In so doing, the deacon is guiding them to follow God's guidelines found in Matthew 18:15–17.

- When a deacon is approached about changes being made, the deacon should listen graciously. After the church member has had the opportunity to vent, the deacon must remind the church member that the changes are being made to promote the transforming gospel of Jesus Christ.
- When a church member approaches a deacon about a divisive issue, if the deacon's opinion differs from that of the church leaders, the deacon should never voice that opinion to the congregant. The deacon's words could be used by the church member to create more tension and substantial division.
- When a church member approaches a deacon about someone else's actions, the deacon should admonish the church member gently. The deacon should then remind them that gossip and slander are opposed to God's ways and are divisive.
- Above all, the deacon should read Matthew 18:15–17 to concerned church members. The deacons should then ask them to commit to discussing their thoughts with no one other than the person they're speaking of. After receiving the commitment, the deacon should let them know they're proud of them. Then pray for them.

CHAPTER 8

Growing as a Deacon

Dr. Stephen C. Rice

Why? Why do you need to grow as a deacon? The church identified you as a mature believer who meets the qualifications for the office of deacon in 1 Timothy 3. The church selected *and* elected you to serve as a deacon, so is growth still needed?

If you own a mirror, you know why! A mere glance at your reflection reminds you of the man you are, not the man your church thinks you are. Although you may be grateful for the level of spiritual maturity you have attained, you still have a long way to go. Since the ultimate goal of spiritual maturity is to become like Jesus, we all need growth. Some of the areas where growth is most essential in the life of a deacon are discipleship, family, leadership, health, and evangelism.

Discipleship

What is a disciple? The word *disciple* is found 267 times in the New Testament. *Disciple* comes from the Greek word *mathetes*, which literally means "learner." Simply put, a Christian disciple is a lifelong learner. I define a *disciple* as follows:

> A person who has come to Jesus for eternal life and has embarked upon the lifelong process of becoming like Jesus and following His leadership.

Being a disciple requires us to be lifelong learners, but such growth does not happen automatically. Granted, we all learn each day simply through observation and experience, but a disciple becomes intentional in his pursuit to becoming like Christ. The apostle Paul exhorts the disciple to "be transformed by the renewal of your mind, that by testing you may discern what is the will of God, what is good and acceptable and perfect" (Rom. 12:2 ESV). Intentional, continual learning is essential to any serious progress toward spiritual maturity. But how? How can we continue to learn throughout life? Here are some practical ways to grow in personal discipleship as a deacon.

Practical Ways to Grow in Discipleship

1. Begin with the Bible.

As a runner, I read the best books and articles I can find about running. I listen to the best running podcasts available. I watch running-related YouTube channels often in my spare time. I even founded a Facebook group called "Runners Helping Runners" to learn more about running. Likewise, as a disciple, I read the best Christian books available so I can learn and grow. Reading books is important, but reading God's Book takes precedence! No other writing can compare to the Bible because it is the Word of God. The apostle Paul reminds us that God gave us the Bible to help us become better disciples.

> All Scripture is breathed out by God and profitable for teaching, for reproof, for correction, and for training in righteousness, that the man of God may be complete, equipped for every good work. (2 Tim. 3:16–17 ESV)

Some people want to read the Bible, but they don't know where to start. When they thumb through the sixty-six books, 1,189 chapters, 23,214 verses, and roughly 622,700 words, they are understandably overwhelmed. Here are some simple Bible reading tips that should help.

- *Read the Bible.* Don't make it complicated. You can literally start reading anywhere, and it will be helpful because God gave it to us for that purpose. The Bible is the Word of God. When God speaks to us through His Word, it is always helpful.
- *Read it through in a year.* A thorough, systematic reading through the entire Bible is a good way to attain a broader understanding. This approach exposes a believer to the entire council of God and guards against instinctively focusing on favorite

passages. Numerous Bible-reading plans exist online and in print, along with multiple Bible-reading apps.

- *Read it slowly during the year.* For several years in a row, I read the entire Bible. The last few years, I have been enriched by reading smaller sections. I read slowly and often read through the same passage several times. Some refer to this as meditating on the Bible. Meditation, in the biblical sense, simply means focused thinking.

- *Listen to the Bible.* Apps allow a person to easily listen to the Bible being read while commuting, cooking, exercising, or just about anywhere you would want. My wife has a thirty-five to forty-five-minute commute each day and finds it helpful to listen to the Bible while driving. I suspect she is even more patient in heavy traffic as a result.

- *Read it with friends.* Although it should not totally replace private Bible reading, reading the Bible with fellow believers can be rewarding. Go into any coffee shop throughout the day, and you will likely see a group of people discussing the Bible with lattes in hand. I know an older group of men who have met weekly for years in a local restaurant to read and discuss the Bible.

- *Read it with family.* Couples and families can benefit by reading together or by following the same plan and discussing their readings along the way.

2. *Read helpful books.*

In addition to the Bible, godly books can help us grow spiritually. Study Bibles that provide good introductions and verse-by-verse notes, devotionals, and Bible commentaries are especially helpful. Books focusing on spiritual disciplines, biblical leadership, theology, and biographies of godly believers are also beneficial. A deacon seeking to be a lifelong learner can benefit by having a reading goal along with a specific plan to reach the goal. Most reading goals focus on the number of books or the number of pages targeted for completion. Depending on your reading speed and available time, you might adopt one of the following reading goals:

- 1 book per month (12 per year)
- 1 book per week (52 per year)
- 1 book per day (365 per year)
- 1 book per year (for those who dislike reading)
- 1 book before you die (for nonreaders)
- 5 pages per day (12 books per year based on 150-page books)
- 10 pages per day (24 books per year based on 150-page books)
- 15 pages per day (36 books per year based on 150-page books)
- 20 pages per day (48 books per year based on 150-page books)
- 25 pages per day (60 books per year based on 150-page books)

In addition to a goal, it is helpful to make a reading list or stack. I usually make both. I make a list of books I plan to read throughout the year and place them on a shelf. I have other books I might read throughout the year if time allows, but they are not a top priority. Throughout the year, new books are released that move into one of these two reading categories. Some readers are inspired by participating in Christian book clubs or by coordinating reading with friends or colleagues. Although it doesn't work for me, some listen to audiobooks as an effective method of learning and growth.

3. Use technology.

Technology can help deacons mature as disciples. Christian podcasts and online sermons provide the listener with teaching from renowned leaders throughout the world. Bible study tools such as Logos allow a lifelong learner to access vast libraries and Bible study tools anywhere the Internet is available. Facebook groups along with apps like GroupMe, WhatsApp, and Slack provide unlimited opportunities to learn and grow in virtual communities. All of this is available to us on a phone or smart device. Often as I listen to someone preaching in person, I scroll on my phone from the text to Bible study tools to read textual or background information that adds to my learning. We should use technology wisely to help us grow and learn.

Family

> A deacon must be faithful to his wife and must manage his children and his household well. (1 Tim. 3:12 NIV)

Because the work of a deacon is so vital to the health of a local church, deacons can be tempted to neglect our biological family to serve our spiritual family. As deacons, we must serve both. It is a necessity and a privilege afforded to us by God, but balance is difficult to discover and more difficult to maintain.

When my children were young and still at home, I drove to the elementary school and picked up my son on his final day of the school year. He was excited for summer vacation, and so was I. "Son, you know what we're going to do this summer?" "What, Dad?" "We're going to play a lot of golf." We both loved to play golf and anticipated many fun rounds together.

At the time I served as pastor of a growing congregation, which meant high demands. A few days later, my son asked, "Dad, are we ready to play golf?" I explained that some matters had come up at church, but we would play soon. A few days later he asked again. I detailed how important the work of the church was and that we would be playing soon.

The week school was scheduled to start, my son said, "Dad, I know you're busy with important work for the church, but you promised that we would play golf this summer. School is about to start, and we haven't played golf one single time." His words broke my heart, and I told him that I was truly sorry.

I went to the main office after school started and told the principal that I needed to check my son out that afternoon for personal reasons. As we walked to the car, my son wondered aloud if something was wrong. I assured him nothing was wrong—everything was just right.

When we got in the car, he asked where we were going. I said, "We're going golfing!" His face lit up with the best smile I can remember. I apologized again for prioritizing the church over my family and promised to do better. We had one of the best afternoons ever on the course. We practically had the place to ourselves because everyone else was at work or in school!

Don't neglect your family! You can't serve God properly as a deacon unless you also serve those who share your last name. Do whatever it takes to find the proper balance between serving the church as a deacon and serving your family. They are one and the same.

Leadership

As we observe the ministry of a deacon, it may prove helpful to look at the broader subject of biblical leadership. Instinctually, any study of biblical leadership must look to the life of Jesus. Jesus was the ultimate leader, and He provided the greatest example of how a leader should lead. Jesus defined leadership by His words and by His lifestyle. We all need to grow in our desire to lead like Jesus. Let's consider three characteristics of the leadership model of Jesus.

1. Jesus led as a servant.

One of the beautiful words in the work of the church is *diakanos*. The word means "service" and is an accurate description of what Christ did for His disciples in the upper room. New Testament leadership is not about flashy, public relations and platform personalities. New Testament leadership is about humble service to the group. For example, in Acts 6, some leaders served the Word while some leaders served tables, but all leaders served.

A few years ago, my family and I watched the show *American Idol*. Being a musical family, we enjoyed the time together listening to excellent young musicians. Ultimately, the American viewers determine who will be the "American Idol" by their votes. Success is defined as winning the show or at least releasing a hit song because of being on the show.

In America, there are many symbols of success. In golf, success is winning one of the major tournaments: The Masters, The U.S. Open, The British Open, or The P.G.A. In baseball, success is winning the *World Series*. In basketball, success is winning the NBA Championship. Our culture often defines success as having the corner office, a good-looking spouse, an expensive sports car, or a huge house.

Have you ever thought about what success looks like in the Bible? In John 13, just hours before His crucifixion, Jesus gave the answer. Wanting to make a lasting impression on His disciples, Jesus provided them with His own symbol of success—the towel.

Success is symbolized by a towel!

So he got up from the meal, took off his outer clothing, and wrapped a towel around his waist. After that, he poured water into a basin and began to wash his disciples' feet, drying them with the towel that was wrapped around him. (John 13:4–5 NIV)

The towel represented *service* and service represented *success*. Although He was the leader and was, in fact, God, Jesus washed the feet of His followers. He performed the act of a household servant. Think about it: if *He* served, so should we. In explaining His actions, He told them:

"I have set you an example that you should do as I have done for you. Very truly I tell you, no servant is greater than his master, nor is a messenger greater than the one who sent him. Now that you know these things, you will be blessed if you do them." (John 13:15–17 NIV)

Late in life, Albert Einstein removed portraits of Newton and Maxwell from his wall and replaced them with portraits of Ghandi and Schweitzer. For Einstein, it was time to replace the image of success with the image of service. Still, Jesus went further by demonstrating that *success is service*! Reacting to the disciples' obvious misconceptions about success, Jesus clearly told them:

"Whoever wants to become great among you must be your servant, and whoever wants to be first must be your slave—just as the Son of Man did not come to be served, but to serve, and to give his life as a ransom for many." (Matt. 20:26–28 NIV)

Jesus clearly demonstrated for the twelve disciples, and for the millions of disciples to follow, that the greatest accomplishment on earth is serving others in the name of the Lord. No position, title, or accomplishment is greater in the eyes of God than service. The top position in the kingdom of God is the position of a humble servant.

This doesn't mean a Christian leader should not strive for excellence. On the contrary, Christian leaders should strive to develop their lives to the best of their ability. They should possess what Ted Engstrom refers to as "sanctified ambition." Ambition can be sinful, but when used to the glory of God, it is praiseworthy.[11]

2. Jesus led as a shepherd.

Jesus said, "I am the good shepherd; I know my sheep and my sheep know me—just as the Father knows me and I know the Father—and I lay down my life for the sheep" (John 10:14–15 NIV). He loved His sheep so much that He laid down His life on their behalf. As the good shepherd, He knew His sheep. Likewise, good leaders know their followers and are willing to sacrifice on their behalf!

I witnessed a modern-day example of a shepherd one day on my father-in-law's farm. I was hitting golf balls in the pasture when I noticed one sheep had wandered away from the flock. The sheep was pacing back and forth between the flock and the creek. As I ventured toward the creek to retrieve a poorly struck golf ball, I heard a lamb near the water. After several minutes of searching, I noticed that the lamb had fallen into the creek and had made his way back to the shoreline. The bank was washed away by the water, so the lamb could not make his way to the top of the bank.

I ran and apprised my father-in-law of the predicament. After arriving at the scene, he quickly assessed the situation. He removed his pants and shirt in the open field. While climbing down the bank, he slipped and fell into the water himself. After gaining some degree of footing on the muddy creek bank, he grabbed the lamb in his arms and tried to hand it to up to me. His feet slipped again, and they both plummeted into the water. He kept the lamb in his arms, made his way to the bank again, and was able to successfully hand him to me on the second attempt.

I helped my father-in-law climb the slippery slope and watched the soaked little lamb run across the field where he joined the sheep that had acted so strangely. The drenched shepherd and I reasoned that she was the mother. Their reunion was dramatic. I was struck that my father-in-law did not concern himself with the opinions of the neighbors when the lamb was in danger. His only concern was to restore the lamb to safety. He publicly removed his cumbersome clothing to rescue the lamb. For me that experience was a vivid picture of the care a shepherd should give his sheep. Jesus set an example every Christian leader should follow.

3. *Jesus led in a surprising way.*

Jesus's attitude toward success and greatness must have seemed strange. It was diametrically opposed to the attitude of the world in which He lived. He said, "Whoever wants to become great among you must be your servant, and whoever wants to be first must be slave of all" (Mark 10:43–44 NIV). In God's view, greatness is not determined by the number of one's servants; greatness is determined by the number one serves.

True greatness and leadership are achieved in selfless service to others instead of the standards given by the world. As important as education is, effective spiritual leadership does not come because of theological training or a seminary degree but rather as a selection by God of those who are prepared by Him for the role of leadership.

Health

For years I've dreamed of running in the historic Boston Marathon. It is the world's oldest annual marathon and is often viewed as the pinnacle of the sport. To run in the race on Patriot's Day in April, a runner must first qualify by running a time on a Boston Qualifying (BQ) certified course that meets an age-graded standard.

In the fall of 2018, I decided on a BQ attempt at the Columbus Marathon in Ohio. Lee Staats, a running friend of mine, volunteered to run the race with me. He successfully qualified for Boston on two prior occasions and was excited about my potential to do so as well. Every marathoner knows there comes a point in the race when you question whether you can continue. During those race "rough" spots, nothing is more helpful than having a buddy running beside you! But for the purpose of a BQ, the only thing that matters is how quickly you *finish* the 26.2-mile course. It doesn't matter how fast you run portions of the race if you do not finish. You *must* complete the distance within the qualifying standards. The Christian life is a lot like a marathon. A lifelong learner should strive to run the race of life well and to completion.

The most infamous portion of the Boston Marathon course is called "Heartbreak Hill." The "hill" only rises eighty vertical feet over a half-mile portion of the race, but the hill comes between miles twenty and twenty-one when the runners are often near exhaustion. Thousands of spectators gather there to cheer on the runners. During one race, a young man was near total exhaustion as he approached Heartbreak Hill. Halfway up the slope, an older man, in better shape, came alongside the younger man. He put his arm around him and quietly encouraged him. Together, step-by-step, they painstakingly climbed. The fitness level of the older man allowed them both to reach the top.

Exercise provides many benefits. You don't have to run; you can walk, hike, cycle, swim, lift weights, shoot hoops, golf—all provide benefits. Exercise produces discipline and clear thinking. It helps you feel better, look better, and act better. Exercise even broadens your gospel prospect pool by bringing you into contact with others in your sport who need Christ.

I have fought the good fight, I have finished the race, I have kept the faith. Henceforth there is laid up for me the crown of righteousness, which the Lord, the righteous judge, will award to me on that day, and not only to me but also to all who have loved his appearing. (2 Tim. 4:7–8 ESV)

Evangelism

The Bible teaches that evangelism was important to Jesus and a key component of the early church. Jesus demonstrated the importance of evangelism at the beginning of His ministry when He visited the synagogue in His home village of Nazareth. He read the following quote from the Old Testament book of Isaiah:

The Spirit of the Lord is on me, because he has anointed me to proclaim good news to the poor. He has sent me to proclaim freedom for the prisoners and recovery of sight for the blind, to set the oppressed free, to proclaim the year of the Lord's favor. (Luke 4:18–19 NIV)

He focused largely on the evangelistic endeavor of spreading good news. He told the people of Capernaum that He had to evangelize other cities (Luke 4:43).

When Jesus called men to be disciples, He told them they would be "fishers of men" (Matt. 4:19 ESV). He demonstrated the priority of evangelism when He said, "Whoever publicly acknowledges me before others, the Son of Man will also acknowledge before the angels of God. But whoever disowns me before others will be disowned before the angels of God" (Luke 12:8–9 NIV).

In the parable of the great banquet, Jesus said, "Go out to the roads and country lanes and compel them to come in, so that my house will be full" (Luke 14:23 NIV). The three parables in Luke 15 stress evangelism by emphasizing the urgency of searching for the lost sheep, the lost coin, and the lost son. Jesus gave the disciples the Great Commission as one of His last commands.

The gospel is good news to those who hear, but many Christians are not involved in telling others the news. If more Christians share the good news of Christ, more people will accept Christ into their lives. Jesus worked hard at spreading the good news, but a lack of workers existed in His day as well. Matthew wrote:

> Jesus went through all the towns and villages, teaching in their synagogues, proclaiming the good news of the kingdom and healing every disease and sickness. When he saw the crowds, he had compassion on them, because they were harassed and helpless, like sheep without a shepherd. Then he said to his disciples, "The harvest is plentiful but the workers are few. Ask the Lord of the harvest, therefore, to send out workers into his harvest field." (Matt. 9:35–38 NIV).

Roy J. Fish and J. E. Conant believed that evangelism was the most important task of the church and that every member of the church should be involved in personal evangelism. They wrote, "The central activity of the church is to witness or to share. Sharing is the main work of the whole church throughout the whole world."[12] I studied evangelism under Fish during the early 1980s. Fish often told the class about evangelistic encounters he had during the days leading up to class. Evangelism was obviously his passion, but it should also be the passion of the local church and of every believer.

God does not expect every person to be involved in the same style or program of evangelism, but He does expect every Christian to be involved in evangelism. A believer is not limited to a specific evangelistic technique, but God calls each Christian to evangelize. Jay Strack and Robert G. Witty wrote:

> As the first-century evangelists spoke and wrote of Jesus to their generation, so must Christians today bring the good news to our needy generation. . . . The church today must be reminded that the Commission is not limited to the early Christians, but rather it is a divine directive to Christians throughout the ages.[13]

Lifestyle Evangelism

A deacon can be involved in different types of evangelism. One type of evangelism is lifestyle evangelism or relational evangelism. With this approach, a deacon shares the gospel with persons with whom he has a relationship. He establishes additional relationships for the distinct purpose of witnessing. Aldrich referred to evangelism as a lifestyle:

> When an individual, a family, or a body of believers are moving together toward wholeness (holiness), a credible lifestyle emerges (blamelessness), and their potential for effective witness (beauty) increases dramatically.

Because this is true, evangelism is a way of living beautifully and opening one's web of relationships to include the nonbeliever.[14]

Oscar Thompson adopted and taught an evangelistic lifestyle approach he called Concentric Circles of Concern. He wrote, "The most important word in the English language, apart from proper nouns, is *relationship*."[15] Throughout the book he stressed the importance of sharing Christ with acquaintances within established circles of relationships without excluding persons outside those relational circles.

Programs of Evangelism

As a young believer, I felt that every believer should be involved in a regular church visitation program. I understand now that every church should have a church visitation program, but most members will not participate. Deacons, however, should participate. By doing so, they lead by example by practicing lifestyle evangelism and participating in the church's program of visitation. Their example shows that they care about the lost, believe in the power of the gospel, and commit to the Great Commission.

Conclusion

What an honor to serve the Lord! What a double honor to serve the Lord's church as a deacon. Serve well as a new deacon but continue to grow. Grow closer to the Lord and become more effective in your role every single year! He deserves it, He desires it, He delights in it, and He demands it. To Him be praise!

Notes

1. A. B. Simpson, "Filled with the Spirit," OChristian, accessed June 15, 2022, http://articles.ochristian.com/article6351.shtml.

2. David Guzik, "1 Timothy—Qualifications for Leaders," Enduring Word, accessed June 15, 2022, https://enduringword.com/bible-commentary/1-timothy-3.

3. Walter A. Elwell, "Ordination," *Baker Encyclopedia of the Bible* (Ada, MI: Baker Publishing, 1988), 1594.

4. A. H. Hodge, *Manual of Forms* (Wentworth Press, 2019).

5. Patrick Lencioni, *Death by Meeting* (Hoboken, NJ: Jossey-Bass, 2004). This is the author's assessment of its content as a PhD expert witness.

6. Stephen Arterburn, *CSB Restoration Bible* (Nashville, TN: Holman, 2018).

7. John R. Bisagno, *Letters to Timothy* (Nashville, TN: B&H, 2001).

8. Les and Leslie Parrott, *Real Relationships: From Bad to Better and Good to Great* (Grand Rapids, MI: Zondervan 2011).

9. John Franklin, *And the Place Was Shaken: How to Lead a Powerful Prayer Meeting* (Nashville, TN: B&H Publishing, 2005), 60–63.

10. Lawrence O. Richards and Gary J. Bredfeldt, *Creative Bible Teaching,* updated, rev. ed. (Chicago, IL: Moody Publishers, 2020).

11. Ted W. Engstrom, *The Making of a Christian Leader* (Grand Rapids, MI: Zondervan, 1978), 38.

12. Roy J. Fish and J. E. Conant, *Every Member Evangelism for Today* (New York: Harper & Row, 1976).

13. Jay Strack and Robert G. Witty, Do the Work of an Evangelist (Nashville, TN: Broadman Press, 1990).

14. Joe Aldrich, *Lifestyle Evangelism: Learning to Open Your Life to Those around You* (Sisters, OR: Multnomah: 2006).

15. Oscar Thompson, *Concentric Circles of Concern: Seven Stages for Making Disciples* (Nashville: B&H, 1999).